GOING HOLLY-WOOD

MARIE BRENNER

GOING HOLLY-WOOD:

An Insider's Look at Power and
Pretense in the Movie Business

DELACORTE PRESS/NEW YORK

Published by
Delacorte Press
1 Dag Hammarskjold Plaza
New York, New York 10017

ACKNOWLEDGMENTS

"Marthe Keller" first published in *Cosmopolitan*, July 1977.

"A Star Is Shorn" reprinted with permission by *New Times*, 1/24/75.

"The Hottest Agent in Hollywood" first published as "Is Sue Mengers Too Pushy for Hollywood?" *New York* magazine, March 17, 1975. Copyright © 1975 by the NYM Corp. Reprinted with the permission of *New York* magazine.

"The New Hollywood Has Arrived. He's Italian" first published as "Dino De Laurentiis Conquers America," *New York* magazine, October 17, 1974. Copyright © 1974 by the NYM Corp. Reprinted with the permission of *New York* magazine.

"When Are We Going to Make a Picture Together?" first published as "Out of the Hollywood Tax Shelters and Into the Trenches with Lester Persky," *New West*, January 31, 1977.

"The Trials of Tom Laughlin" first published as "Who Does Tom Laughlin Think He Is?," *New York* magazine, August 4, 1975. Copyright © 1975 by the NYM Corp. Reprinted with the permission of *New York* magazine.

"Final Tribute: *Cher*" reprinted with the permission of *New Times*, 2/26/76.

"Whatever Happened to Ali MacGraw?" first published in *Redbook*, February 1976.

LIBRARY OF CONGRESS CATALOGING IN PUBLICATION DATA

Brenner, Marie.
Going Hollywood.

1. Moving-picture industry—California—
Hollywood—Addresses, essays, lectures. I. Title.
PN1993.5.U65B68   791.43'0973   77-24564
ISBN 0-440-03018-8

For Jesse Kornbluth,
my best editor and friend

Contents

GOING
HOLLYWOOD

The tradition of Evelyn Waugh, Scott Fitzgerald, Raymond Chandler, and Nathanael West holds that Los Angeles is a cultural wasteland with the personality of a paper cup. It's an understandable conclusion. New York's creative exiles have traditionally courted and scorned the place where you can keep your tan as you get rich—forty years ago, on her arrival in L.A., Mae West haughtily announced to the Hollywood press corps, "I made it in New York, boys, so I can *certainly* make it here"—and the journalists who have flown in and out like hit men never cease to be amazed by the town's provincialism. These East Coast writers, who have, until recently, produced most of the consequential writing about Hollywood, generally return home proclaiming two great truths: The Polo Lounge is full of old men in white shoes and art directors in sideburns, and Hollywood is dead.

Two years ago I moved to Los Angeles, not quite as deliberately as Thoreau retreated to Walden Pond. I did not believe Hollywood would be a rich and complex tapestry, swarming with life the in-and-outers never got to see, nor did I agree the town was as moribund and decadent as most reports from this front seemed to suggest. I thought the scene was simply underreported, that no recent writers save Joan Didion and her husband, John Gregory Dunne, had taken the time to hang around long enough to identify the players and observe their moves. Perhaps for the briefest of moments I even imagined that bringing a form of investigative reporting to Hollywood might not be such a bad way to earn a living, but now I'm not sure of that one. I am sure I was very naive.

I did learn one thing in Hollywood: There's a reason why they call it "The Coast." And it's not because the movie business is on its final downward slide, as the jeremiads of the New York film critics' minyan would have you believe. "Hollywood has fallen into the Pacific," one critic intoned at a recent screening, by way of explaining away another terrible insult to the moviegoing public. He's wrong—Hollywood is neither tumbling into Santa Monica Bay nor preparing to be swallowed in the Great Earthquake. What's happening in Hollywood seems more like a lateral slide, a shuffling two-step danced to the music of the Hustle—quite literally, a coast, a dignified and stately approach to frenzy.

Now this isn't exactly the freshest news. "The business"—as Hollywood refers to itself—has been mired in the slime ever since it was raped by the Justice Department twenty-five years ago; the studios' forced divestiture of their theaters eliminated their security blanket and made productivity as uncertain as profit. Without the guaranteed income from the theaters, and with the new competition from television, the movie business quickly sank into what appeared to be a state of terminal disease. But the patient didn't die, and, buoyed by what may be permanent remission, the studios continue to play for big stakes, praying that back-to-back blockbusters will cure things once and for all. Thus, in a time when there are fewer films, more of them tend to be $26-million babies like *King Kong* and $14-million clunkers like *Lucky Lady.* Ask what happened to the small film, the art film, the "personal" film, and a studio executive reels off the bottom-line truth of movie financing. Even a smallish film tends to run $4 million these days, what with the stars' astronomical salaries, the producers' exorbitant fees, union contracts, and studio overhead.

What is news, as Marvin Goldman, president of the National Organization of Theater Owners, explains, is that "everyone's swinging for the fences. All they want is home runs, a few pictures that can bring in huge grosses." That decision has cost Goldman some of his membership. Along with smaller chains that have folded, the Walter Reade Organization—which had twenty-nine theaters in "major markets"—recently declared bankruptcy, blaming the scarcity of product. The studios' ever-escalating demands for cash up front and guaranteed bookings are certain to reduce the number of theaters still more, however much money they bring into the studios' coffers.

These are the signs of bloodletting, of desperate decisions designed to keep red ink away for another year, regardless of the long-term effect on the industry. The New York City theaters are filled with revivals, and Radio City Music Hall, for thirty years a tourist mecca, has had to resort to rock concerts and gospel shows to keep its doors open on those increasingly infrequent weeks when there's a real G-rated film to be shown.

The result of these eleventh-hour ploys is hardening audience resistance to films in general. Last year's intended blockbusters—*Lucky Lady, The Hindenburg, Buffalo Bill and the Indians,* and *The Missouri Breaks*—flopped within weeks of their premieres. *Black Sunday, Islands in the Stream,* and *Marathon Man*—Paramount's triple entry in this year's blockbuster stakes—will hardly turn corporate ink from red to black. Overall movie attendance has dropped 10 percent from 1975. Still, Hollywood refuses to learn its lesson, and more producers resolve to go broke underestimating the public while creators of marginally original films like *Taxi Driver* and *Network* have found themselves with major hits. Not so paradoxically, these films' financial success earns them a reputation for being, if not "art," at least wildly inventive. This is hardly great praise in a New Hollywood of *Airports* and sequels-of-sequels. In this New Hollywood, the producers of *Jaws* celebrate their nine-figure gross not by making more rarefied films, but by serving up more *Jaws,* and worse: a remake of *Gone With the Wind!*

More deserving of notice is that a *Network* or a *Taxi Driver,* both serious and worthwhile films, should earn money—as well as praise. With the emphasis on $100-million grosses and formula films, movies that the money men intuit would be "difficult"—lacking in commercial appeal—are more commonly dumped into second-run release patterns before they've had a chance to find any audience at all. That *The Late Show* and *Rocky* escaped this treatment is more a credit to the tenacity of their creators rather than to any lobbying on the part of their studios. Meanwhile, failed veterans get deals that should go to promising newcomers, and the government has dealt the next generation of filmmakers a body blow by eliminating film tax-shelters.

These are True Facts, all right, but I have not come to shovel another spadeful on the Hollywood corpse, or kick those few zombies who are walking around with the assumption it's still alive. The smell of death may be as pervasive in Los Angeles as three-hour dry cleaners and

Going Hollywood

Pup N'Taco stands, but the quality of death isn't a subject that held my attention for long. What actually replaced making movies—and I don't mean TV or rock-and-roll, the industries with speeded-up production schedules which rightly claim to shape public taste, and respond to it, faster and more significantly than films—was what finally drew my attention, continues to hold it, and leaves me limp with wonder.

What has replaced making movies is the movie makers' obsession with power. That struggle for power is as ingrained-American as Gary Cooper's white hat, so why should anyone be surprised by such an obvious truth? Because, though Hollywood product is still vital to the nation's fantasies, Hollywood power is almost chimerical. In a depressed industry there's precious little of the real stuff, and it's parceled out so sparingly that you'd have a better shot at writing the next *Jaws* than getting hold of it. So power in Hollywood has come to mean something else: buying and keeping a place at the table, maintaining some respectable position in the pecking order. To an industry that cannot recover its potency, the illusion of power is as good as the thing itself.

Consider a production vice-president at the most active studio in Hollywood. He makes perhaps $150,000 a year—with bonuses, $200,000. In a time when executives pass in and out of studios as if their offices were equipped with revolving doors, he has, like Faulkner's Dilsey, "endured." He works late, but his marriage is good, and he plays tennis on courts with men more anxious to stroke him than the ball. He has—people think he has—power. Then a potential deal comes along.

Let us say—because this is how it really happened—the project in question is Judith Rossner's *Looking for Mr. Goodbar.* A producer alerts him that the book/project

Marie Brenner

/basic material is coming up for auction, and pitches an approach which solves the big hole in the novel: how to develop the character of the killer. The studio executive commits his studio to the acquisition of *Mr. Goodbar* "at any cost." The producer crosses his fingers and prays that no other production head is making the same promise to another filmmaker across town.

On the day of the auction, the producer cannot restrain himself. He has his secretary put in a call to the production executive's office—he wants to know how high the studio will bid for *Mr. Goodbar.* The vice-president's secretary assures the producer that her boss is "in the air" between New York and L.A. Right now he is over Oklahoma, but he'll arrive at L.A. International around two, and his first call will be to Rossner's agent.

The producer is reassured. He does not know he is getting the Continental Travel gambit, an old power move.

At four, the production vice-president still hasn't landed. His secretary isn't worried, though; she knows he'll pull through. And even in "the city of one-night stands" it's inconceivable that her boss—so vital, so ruggedly handsome, with squint lines that broadcast his sensitivity and depth—is lying in some Oklahoma cornfield, the papers in his shattered briefcase strewn by the spring wind. No, he's simply lying. He's locked in his office, developing other projects, unable to deal with reality by telling the agent the truth: "The book's not a best-seller yet, so the head of the studio won't allow me to bid up to $250,000 for it," is the line the vice-president was neglecting to say. He couldn't. To display any sign of possible weakness to "the community" would be worse than bad form—it would be a giant step backward. Only a fool would self-destruct like that when he could take the Hollywood Powder and preserve his status as an executive with Real Power.

The truth is, like any hustling producer, the studio vice-president is struggling to pass go. Literally: Nothing is so valued as a "go project," a deal which has survived not only the initial development stage but also a second- and third-draft screenplay, a few anonymous script doctors, an actual production commitment from one or more of Hollywood's five stars, and—the very term sends chills—an actual "start date." A film's eventual profits are only a side issue. The moment a project gets a go, the heavens open: Studio office space and WATS lines, even studio-supplied secretaries appear. The producer starts to collect most of his $250,000 producing fee, the stars each get their million, and the director will begin to turn upward of $300,000 over to his accountants. This sacrilege is what's known as above-the-line costs. "Below the line" includes what the studio audaciously calls the million dollars it will insist on receiving for "prints and advertising," in addition to its distribution fee. No matter if the movie bombs; few lucky enough to be on either side of that magic bottom line will come out as losers. Once this is understood, there is little more that anyone needs to know about a studio's accounting system. It won't even seem surprising that for a movie to *make* money it needs to recoup just about three times the cost of making it in the first place.

There are plenty of other paradoxes, but outsiders most frequently get hung up on the central one. For every ten announcements of a just-made movie deal, one of those projects will be lucky enough to wind up on the screen. Clearly, a logical question follows: Why would anyone waste that degree of time and money putting films "in development" when seemingly there isn't sufficient money to produce them or no real enthusiasm for distributing and promoting them?

In the fall of 1974, the Paramount development list indicated that thirty-one projects were being prepared for the big screen. Bob Evans's $400,000 splurge on Dorothy Uhnack's *Law and Order* (it would later wind up on TV) was there, as was Frank Yablans's almost equally expensive tome about Martin Bormann. The Yablans project was less likely to get on—his press conference announcing the Nazi film was followed by an interview in *The New York Times* in which he revealed his desire to run for President—but it still had a better shot than the majority of books and screenplays, which had been bought for much less money. As it worked out, Yablans was squeezed out of his job by Gulf + Western chief Charles Bluhdorn, and Bob Evans left Paramount to become an independent producer. Of the forty-nine other projects making their way across the Pacific Styx, almost all of them fell by the wayside long before they were in danger of going into production.

Paramount isn't the only studio with a morgue the size of the Ritz. Over at Warner's, they've canceled plans for filming Jay Presson Allen's *Just Tell Me What You Want*—a tome acquired for half a million dollars. Sylvia Wallace's *The Fountains* died there too, but that one set the studio back only a quarter of a million dollars. United Artists still mourns the $400,000 it spent on *Couples.* Columbia blew $300,000 when it aborted Joseph Wambaugh's *The Onion Field,* and back at the Paramount lot they're still shaking their heads over Bob Evans's $2-million purchase of the play *Coco,* as well as Stanley Jaffe's $150,000 spree for Paige Mitchell's *The Covenant.* It is not on record that anyone is particularly surprised by the waste of money and this remarkable failure-to-success ratio, but we may assume that very few real producers are ever convinced a studio intends to "move forward" on their projects.

If there is a conspiracy afoot in Hollywood, it's a tacit one between the studio executives—mostly former agents and entertainment lawyers—and the agents and lawyers who bring projects to them, knowing that all the hype and pressure in the world can really produce little more significant than . . . a development deal. In Hollywood today, a deal is certification enough; it gives the financial element the illusion of activity and the "creative element" the delusion of participation. Like the quality of mercy, it is thus twice blessed.

This is, however, not a minor-league, cozy arrangement that makes everyone a low-stakes winner. Once you have joined the ranks of those who either make or have deals, it becomes a matter of great consequence Who You Are. If you have $9 million from the Syrian government and your name is Moustapha Akkad, you can make —on your own—*Mohammed, Messenger of God.* If you have guts and dozens of family friends back in Brooklyn who'll kick in a thousand dollars apiece, you can—like young director Marty Davidson—put together *Lords of Flatbush,* then sell your film to Columbia Pictures, bringing your investors eventual profits of 1,200 percent. But if you are like most of your peers in the producers' ranks—unwilling or unable to come up with a few easy million—then you have to hustle. The line forms at the studio.

So how do you pass go? The rules are arbitrary and ever-changing, and there is much disagreement whether the game exists at all, but, regardless of their ambivalences, few refrain from trying to play the personality game. In the New Hollywood, it is the closest most people ever will come to genuine power.

Marie Brenner

Sometimes it even works. Francis Ford Coppola is both a personality and a moneymaker, so his $20-million expenditure on *Apocalypse Now* goes unquestioned.* Ditto Julia Phillips's equally expensive *Close Encounters of the Third Kind.* The difference isn't in the profiles of the filmmakers—Coppola and Phillips both have high visibility within the industry—but that Phillips's movie is backed by Columbia Pictures and Coppola is with the currently hot United Artists. Columbia is reliably reported to be in perilous financial shape, and that $20 million for *Close Encounters* represents just about their last chips; with a break-even point of some $55 million, the backers of this film are certainly betting against the house. So why would Columbia be making the film? The answer—and this will be disputed—seems obvious. *Close Encounters* sports not just one A player, but two. Its director is Steven Spielberg, *Jaws* wunderkind and Hollywood hero of the year, who mastered the Hollywood idiom at 27—an even more precocious age than Peter Bogdanovich's first triumph. An executive can easily rationalize that expense away. So with the help of flying saucers (*Close Encounters* is about extraterrestrial contact), he may just be able to save Columbia Pictures. And—there's always an and—should Spielberg rescue Columbia from its army of creditors, he will ascend in true Hollywood style: The wunderkind director who was denied an Oscar nomination for *Jaws* will suddenly be anointed as a genuine *auteur*, even . . . a Star Person.

Thus it was possible recently for two producers working on a small film to fight over their relative merits as

*But even these moneymakers are not allowed to clean out the bank. *Apocalypse Now*—plagued by typhoons, disease, an ever-soaring shooting schedule that doubled its cost—was finished only because Francis Coppola decided to invest almost his entire personal fortune to complete the film.

people. While their stars waited on the set, the inveterate partygoer and celebrity collector pulled his more diligent partner aside, walking him to a deserted vineyard so they could have it out once and for all. You're bothering me with these incessant calls to the set, the partygoer complained. They're annoying when I'm out making deals for us. His partner disagreed; to his mind, he was doing all the work while his partner claimed the credit. The partyhound exploded: "Do you know what's wrong with you? Do you know why you'll never make it in this town? Because you are not a *Star Person.* Bob Evans is a Star Person. Sue Mengers is a Star Person. Barry Diller is a Star Person. I am a Star Person—and only Star People can make it big here."

A year later, the Star Person gave up his $800-a-month apartment and leased Mercedes for a $200 flat looking up at the Hollywood Hills. For a few extra dollars a month, the phone company gave him a number ending in double zero, so he can answer his calls as if he were at his office and his secretary just happened to be out. But that decline in his fortunes doesn't matter. He has a new deal. And he hasn't had to miss a party to get it.

It is much better, apparently, to be a Star Person— even if, as Sue Mengers phrased it, your nose is always pressed against the outside of the bakery window—than it is to be an actual star. Stars fade, but Star People go on forever, hustling in all directions, given that so many of them seem to lack what their human-potential gurus call a "center," a core personality that would suggest there are better ways to conduct a life than to make the emotional equation: ego equals career. For these star persons, the playing becomes the thing—as well as incessant, aimless motion, and connections, and small controversies blown out of proportion. As entertainment lawyer Tom Pollock sees it, "It's like the game of Life we used to kill rainy afternoons with as kids. You pick a combination of points: money, power, love, and fame. You assign the number of points you want to give to each of these qualities. If your choices don't get you around the game board, you have to switch priorities. The people who work in Hollywood are like that. The studio executives get some power but no real money, so they're not happy. They leave to be independent producers—to get money—but they trade off power to get it. They're not happy as producers and not happy as studio heads."

The constant skittering back and forth between roles, with sellers becoming buyers at any moment, keeps people from expressing what they actually might feel about one another. A writer fires his agent warily, knowing they'll meet again when the agent is at a studio—or work with greater intimacy when the agent turns producer and discovers that the client for whom he couldn't get a TV-movie rewrite is suddenly holding a very hot screenplay. Paranoia flourishes in this hothouse atmosphere, and it's not an irrational phobia. If you want a place at the table, it's little more than good business sense to realize that you've got to push through the mob that separates you from the action; even a Francis Coppola has to cultivate personal relationships. Those who haven't kept their friendships in repair (in Hollywood every person one does business with is a friend until shortly after the ink dries) suffer. The case of International Creative Management's former president, Freddie Fields, underscores the point. Fields was an important man—his agency represented Hollywood's brightest stars—so no one was too surprised when Paramount offered him a producing contract of $400,000 a year. The implicit promise was that Fields would deliver his stable—Streisand,

McQueen, Cher, Ryan O'Neal—and Paramount would wind up with a cluster of potentially blockbusting films. Two years and $800,000 later, not one of Fields' ex-stable had appeared in any of his movies. What has Fields' tenure done for Paramount? So far it's produced a pair of small but forgettable films: *Lipstick,* which bombed within days of its release, and *CB,* on which the jury is still out. He has high hopes for *Looking for Mr. Goodbar,* though.

If salaries don't corrupt, then being handed a particle of power does absolutely, sometimes causing the powerful to self-destruct in the process. Former Paramount vice-president Richard Sylbert once talked to me in an interview about his close friend and mentor Mike Nichols. Nichols had had a decline in fortunes; Sylbert— thanks to his decade-long apprenticeship under Mike Nichols—was momentarily on the upswing. So wasn't this the perfect moment for him to say, "Gee, Mike is very depressed. I told him he should never do *The Fortune.* I hope he pulls himself together." At the time Sylbert was confiding this in his sunny office on the Paramount lot, his former mentor was across the country directing the soon-to-be-hit play *Streamers.*

The accusatory weapon of depression-aggression has been wielded against Stanley Donen *(Funny Face, Charade)* as well. Donen's former agent was heard remarking about his client, "I think Stanley is having a breakdown," just because Donen had made the astounding decision to find a new agent. The hostility hidden in remarks like these somehow passes for manifestations of friendship among the moviemakers. It was explained to me thusly: If you have accused someone of "breaking down" or otherwise being locked in an emotional hellhole, you're safe. Not only have you retained your up-to-the-minute awareness of the nuances of the genius's mind-set (your hip quotient), but should the basket case turn around and be involved in a blockbuster film, at least you haven't uttered the Hollywood last rites: "—— will never work again" or "——'s over." Your rancor can simply pass for Deep Concern. This is, after all, the way concerned friends sometimes *do* actually behave.

What didn't pass as the behavior of a concerned friend was a certain vice-president's habit of lecturing to then-Paramount producer (and Oscar winner) David Picker *(Lenny)* on the Fine Art of Making Movies. Picker, who soon ascended to the Paramount presidency, had the good manners to wait several months before replacing his former teacher with a man whose creative concepts meshed more harmoniously with his own. And sometimes even being controversial and/or arrogant can also bring karmic revenge. The line on Hollywood's Star Woman Producer goes like this: "Just wait till her next film bombs. She's fucked over so many people that nobody will take her calls. She won't have a friend left in this town."

(An aside: "This town" is cosmic geography which is applied loosely to describe any location where movies are made, no matter on what part of the globe the moviemaker happens to be. Thus, Run Run Shaw and Sir Lew Grade speaking simultaneously in Hong Kong and London can call filmland "this town" and be referring to exactly the same psychic spot.)

It's hard to think of a business that does less of its real business in offices. Bob Evans's screenings and Sue Mengers's dinners are prize tickets if your ambition is to make not just a deal, but the right deal. The wrong deal is any deal offered to you by a former dress manufacturer, age twenty-eight, who tells you he has nineteen

Going Hollywood

projects "in development" and he's best friends with Sid Sheinberg, Dennis Stanfill, Ted Ashley, Barry Diller, David Begelman, and Mike Medavoy, and that this driving-the-cab thing is only temporary until he gets a commitment from Jane Fonda. The right deal is any deal offered to you by the cabdriver's supposedly intimate friends, since they are the heads of Universal, Twentieth Century–Fox, Warner Brothers, Paramount, Columbia, and United Artists, respectively. If you're walking down the street, a little "basic material" under your arm, and Barbra Streisand or Sidney Lumet or Sydney Pollack or George Roy Hill or Steve McQueen or Al Pacino or Diana Ross or Francis Coppola offers you a ride, take it. Ask your driver to take you to one of the aforementioned studio heads, pull him or her in by the collar (that's known as getting a commitment) and walk out with, *mirabile dictu,* a deal—and the right kind of deal. That process, "getting into bed" (or the car, or even a coffin) with one of these "bankable elements"—either director, or star—makes you a packager. And the right kind of package gets you the right kind of deals. In Hollywood, the best things never come in small packages. You need not grimace in the mirror in the Michael Korda power-mouth position, or favor Korda's sharkskin heel protectors (unless you want to become a New York publishing power), so long as you have some proximity to people who can say, if not yes, then at least a strong maybe. Where to find them? On the studio level, no "maybe" can be given unless a title has a vice which precedes it. Being talented helps you to get access, but it's certainly not mandatory; as dozens of careers attest, all the talent in the universe won't help you if you're not standing around when Producer X is looking for a writer, any writer, or a director, any director, and an agent presses your flesh and finds to his or her delight that there's still a pulse.

As you may suspect, but few admit, what actually goes into making movies has more to do with social intangibles and idiot chance than any aesthetic lessons to be gleaned from a genuine *auteur.* Once you accept that fact, the Hollywood parade takes on a humorous tint, a kind of black-humor devil-may-care *esprit.* David Geffen, who built Asylum Records before moving on to movies at Warner Brothers, is considered "over" at this writing— though he has probably made ten million dollars in the last few years, enough to buy him a controlling interest in Columbia Pictures, should he covet it. William Goldman, who has reigned as the hottest writer in Hollywood for an unprecedented decade, cannot consider working for less than his standard $500,000 a script lest he risk his reputation; thanks to his correct understanding of Hollywood power, *Marathon Man* producer Bob Evans asked Goldman to go to Paramount chief Barry Diller and beg him to grant Sir Laurence Olivier a $10,000 raise. In that situation, the screenwriter-superstar wields more power than the former Paramount executive. Even after Francis Coppola agreed to produce *American Graffiti* and George Lucas delivered his flawless little film to Universal on a $900,000 budget, it sat on the shelf for six months. When it was finally released and grossed a higher earnings-to-cost ratio than any other film in history, there was no scarcity of executives willing to take responsibility.* Only one executive at Warner Brothers, Paula Weinstein—the lone woman, as it turns out—ar-

*Lucas himself was described as "astounded" by *Star Wars,* his recent block-buster. "He was depressed the entire time he was shooting it," a friend said. "And now that it's such a hit, he's gone to Hawaii to recover from shock."

gued for the studio to promote *The Late Show.* Over at Columbia, the executives almost let *Taxi Driver* be released by Universal because they weren't sure if it would turn a dollar if the ratings board gave it an X. (*Taxi Driver* will end up making about $50 million, albeit with an R rating.)

In a seat-of-the-pants business, instinct is all that counts, though few have the nerve to proclaim themselves seers in any of these decisions, which are made either by committee or, more often than not, by the conglomerate hatchet man himself. After they're made, a $150,000-a-year-man delivers the news, and people who don't know better actually think he locked himself in an office the size of an ocean liner, did some TM to focus his decision-making brain center, then rendered judgment like Solomon. If only it worked that way!

Here's how a recent picture—a very successful picture —got made. The producer was a young comer a few years back, bringing out two hits before his thirty-second birthday, even serving a brief tenure as a studio chief. It was his good fortune during that stint to have *Love Story* in production. It was his bad luck to have an altercation with Ryan O'Neal, then a minor TV actor, and inform him that he would never work again in films.

Fade out the studio chief, fade in Ryan O'Neal. It is four years later, and although O'Neal hasn't been in a hit for a year or so, he is unquestionably much more a Star Person than his boy-wonder producer, who has troubles getting his calls returned. Still, the producer gets around. Unfortunately, he gets around Ryan O'Neal at a party in the Hollywood Hills. Now it is O'Neal's turn to play the heavy, especially because the producer, with perfect Hollywood amnesia, remembers not a word of their contretemps. He greets O'Neal warmly—and is astonished when O'Neal flings him against a wall, bashing his head against the stucco while he warns his daughter never to work for this "little ———."

Winter turns to spring, and the producer begs the conglomerate head for mercy. He is handed a picture, his first in years. It's a small film—the subject is kids' baseball—and there are no stars, but it's an in, and he's raring to do it. Then the studio has a change of heart: Find two bankable stars within a month, the producer is told, or forget the picture. This is a monumental challenge, equal to demanding of an atheist that he part the Red Sea, but the producer plunges ahead, signing Walter Matthau for money that puts the film out of small-budget range. Now all he needs is a child star. Unfortunately, there is only one: Tatum O'Neal.

Logically, the project should fall apart at this point; there is no way the producer can sign this star, not when her father has retired her from working with any director other than Peter Bogdanovich. Yet he does, and though her salary ($350,000) and her percentage border on the outrageous, that is not, insiders say, the reason why Tatum O'Neal signed to do *The Bad News Bears.* The reason: Anouk Aimée was coming to L.A. to be with Ryan for the summer. Paramount's big summer movie got made because Tatum O'Neal preferred a sound stage to summer camp.

And the producer? He went to Columbia as head of production. This surprised nobody who understood the way it works. Nary an eyebrow was raised when the new head of production bragged to the *Hollywood Reporter* that he had developed both *The Godfather* and *Love Story* —which he most definitely did not. What did cause minor consternation was the new head of production's phone call to the head of Paramount. "Why are you ruining the distribution of *my* movie?" he snarled some time after *The Bad News Bears* had crossed the $30-million mark. What goes around comes around, and months later he was bounced onto the lot as an "indi prod," a demotion that can't last; within minutes he should be head of production somewhere else. Hell, he'll probably give Ryan O'Neal his shot at directing when he gets there. And that movie will probably outgross *Jaws.*

The perfectly crafted film *The Sting* was perfectly crafted not because of some grand design, but because of a vicious personal fight screenwriter William Goldman and director George Roy Hill got into while they were working on *The Great Waldo Pepper.* That movie suddenly "derailed," as Goldman put it, only to be made two years later. And the director just as suddenly found himself unemployed. Fortunately for George Roy Hill, Universal was making a low-budget film about two con men; Peter Boyle had already been cast. Unfortunately for Peter Boyle, *The Sting*'s brand-new director, George Roy Hill, replaced him with Paul Newman. Then Robert Redford was brought in. The Goldman-Hill fight wound up being directly responsible for the worldwide $100-million gross on *The Sting,* and its producers wound up winning an Academy Award.

It's a great, wonderfully wacky business, the hypester might conclude, but to the journalist who's never witnessed such behavior before or since, it's more like Upward Failure at work. In a closed community, this tendency is hardly surprising; insiders routinely smooth the way for other insiders who can demonstrate that if they are not inordinately competent, at least they aren't threatening to the structure. It's all about survival—staying out of the line of fire. "We don't like strangers here," Cecelia Brady said in *The Last Tycoon.*

But some strangers who understand Hollywood's unwritten laws can slip through, be atomized, and be em-
braced by "the community." Success helps. A film director who was, the story goes, first discovered curled up on
a bench in Echo Park will be directing his third blood-
and-gutser for Warner Brothers this fall. That film was
conceived in a Beverly Hills office decorated with Richard Lindner tapestries and dozens of stills of eviscerated
rectums; the park-bench alumnus called his photo collec-
tion "the basic material" in the same ponderous tone he
used when he compared himself to Jean-Luc Godard.
Somehow, in the context of L.A. it all makes sense. A
young producer of two hit films is routinely barred from
his own sets; he's a creep, and that's exactly the point.
His directors won't let him on their sound stages mainly
because he's "in breach" of an undefined social code.
This producer may have two hit films to his credit, but
he'll never be a Star Person; thus, in Hollywood terms,
he'll always be outside. Power eludes him now, and it will
continue to.

Nobody understands this arcane psychology better
than the second generation, those socialites and Hollywood survivors barricaded in their Beverly Hills houses
behind the hedges which bloom year round. Their re-
ward for remaining in the land where their fathers made
movies as well as deals is one of keeping the torch alive:
If they can't act, they can at least endorse. *Easy Rider*
producer Bert Schneider, at the height of his political
frenzy, can shriek, "The fuckin' working class has to get
off its fuckin' ass," but he's not moving out of his mansion on Mulholland Drive to say it. Schneider's father,
the former head of Columbia Pictures, would approve.
In Hollywood, the son-in-law still rises. And so do his
sisters, brothers, and cousins. They may not run studios,

but they're directing, acting, and trying—like everybody else—to "get it on" while killing time. The difference is that once they get one thing on, these survivors achieve a Second Coming; rewarded by fatter deals, a studio vice-presidency, best-sellerdom, their birthright returns. They also get to make a lot of deals.

So everybody—survivors, scramblers, hustlers, and hypesters—is busy in Hollywood these days, busy as bears before the first snows of winter. So many candidates who want to winter in the cave! The interviews start in the morning and last until dark, with scarcely enough time to slip off for a quick set or two. At night there are screenings and dinners, with nothing ending later than ten thirty, because this is—as they've been saying all along—a working community. And sometimes, for whole months at a time, there are actually movies to be made and the endless, exhausting work of filmmaking before the return to shadowboxing with deals, incessant meetings, and weekends leaden with scripts to read. Make no mistake. This shadowboxing is hard work. It's as laborious and exhausting as ditchdigging to its practitioners, and worse, because it never lets up. The lonely-on-the-way-up stories which would cloy on *Mary Hartman* resonate when heard in Holmby Hills; neuroses brandished in Bel-Air somehow become a logical part of the *angst* of the *plaz.*

Joan Didion coined the contemporary Hollywood metaphor—the deal-is-the-true-art-form—but perhaps we're even a level further removed now, with neuroses as the new standard of Hollywood success. The days of Perrier and roses, with every studio executive crying "Everything's wonderful" before he's locked into Cedars-Sinai with bleeding ulcers, are still with us, will always be with us. Hollywood is a town of bluffers; every-

body likes to pretend to have the goods, a royal flush.*
But something new's afoot: Pain is a trading point. All
over, you hear the power mavens kvetching, even in the
press. The Bob Evanses find it endearing to mention the
Valium and Nembutal combinations that soothe their
traumatized days; the Valerie Harpers nonchalantly sign
their souls over to the est laundromat, as if they're just
another day's load of emotional wash; the John Travoltas
credit the Scientology crusaders. As the rabbi of the
Synagogue of the Performing Arts said to me, "All the
stars come here, because they know if they went to shul
with real people, they probably couldn't get into their
feelings." It's not unusual for the clients of the most
powerful lady agent in Hollywood to hear about her
marital problems; what is surprising is to hear a writer
like Paul Shrader or an actor like Robert De Niro ask to
be judged solely on his work.

I did not find many Shraders or De Niros, though, and
after a while my pieces were done and there was no
longer a reason to stay in Hollywood. I had a hard time
leaving; I think I feared coming back to a world that had
real politics and more tangible problems. I kept thinking
that if I stayed a little longer, I could get more of the
hang of the place. Anyway, I put off coming back; I
wanted to find a reason more complex than the instinctual grabbing for power to connect what I had written.
I wanted to be able to understand Hollywood better than
I did, better even than Cecelia Brady, whose understanding came in "glimmers and in flashes." But I never did,

---

*The classic Hollywood "everything's-wonderful" story is one told by screen-
writer Josh Greenfield: "A friend of mine knew a Hollywood writer who had
cancer and was receiving cobalt treatment. He ran into the writer at a cocktail
party and asked him how the treatment was coming along.

" 'Treatment?' said the writer. 'We're into script.' "

and now that I am away from it, I am suspicious of any belated tendency to find an overview.

Anyway, I've decided Cecelia Brady was right. The profiles I've included are a representative sampling—but just a sampling nonetheless—of those glimmers and flashes which best illustrate the spectrum of Hollywood's reactions to success and power. This is not a narrow range: There are those who are shocked by discovering that the brass ring can be sizzling hot to those who try to force the brass ring down their detractors' throats; there are those who simply want more of what they've got and some—admittedly very few—who simply want to be good at what they do. I consider these pieces as reports from a front, detailed reports in some cases, but reports nonetheless. The common thread, were I to be forced to find one, would have something to do with Hollywood's great guilt trip: people making all that money at jobs which should pay far less. They're never quite sure what they've done to deserve it or when it's going to be stripped away, so they opt to keep on hoping: for the one deal that *will* get made, for another picture, another client, a few more percentage points.

Of course . . . there are exceptions. Some of the "bankables" have taken to producing, although still within the confines of the studio process. Robert Redford deserves credit for his elegant production of *All The President's Men;* Dustin Hoffman put together *Straight Time.* The phenomenon of Warren Beatty as a producer *(Shampoo)* is fascinating, as is the decision of Robert Towne, Beatty's (and Bob Evans's) favorite screenwriter, to work for a studio. John Frankenheimer's directorial comeback with *Black Sunday* might have deserved chronicling, and I, for one, would have been interested in watching George Lucas direct *Star Wars.* Certainly, as a writer I'd have liked to bear witness to the brilliantly engineered writing careers of William Goldman and Paul Shrader.

But the pollster can knock on only so many doors. And what this pollster found was a mixture of those who—in the Hollywood power game—were in various stages of before and after. There were some—like actress Marthe Keller, actor Robert De Niro—on their way all the way up. There were some who had recently arrived—like superstar agent Sue Mengers and film financier Lester Persky, and even the Streisand-Peterses—who hadn't yet perfected how to stop trying so hard. And there were some—like *Billy Jack*'s Tom Laughlin and Cher—who once had had it all, but were slipping, whose momentum was gone.

Underneath the glossiness of their self-deception, I doubt that most of the subjects of these profiles have a clue why they've gotten where they are or even that they might lose what they get. They have become stars only to find themselves in some way victimized by their celebrity; they have sought power only to discover that it really doesn't exist. All they can be sure of is that in spite of all their drive and calculation, in spite of their training and dumb luck, they are still bit players in a larger drama—and what gets on the screen is, for any observer, the least dramatic part of the Hollywood process.

April 1977
New York City

ON THE
WAY UP

NELSON

ROBERT DE NIRO

For a moment, he just stood there, watching, waiting. Nobody on the tree-shaded patio of the Polo Lounge had noticed him yet, perhaps because the slightly built man had emerged from the Beverly Hills Hotel so silently that he seemed not to have stepped onto the terrace as much as always been there. A strikingly dressed Caribbean woman was by his side. With her ethnic clothes and crimped raven hair, it was this woman who drew the stares. Her companion, by comparison, was nondescript: medium height, average weight, dark hair. With the sunlight streaming down on him, he looked like just another man waiting patiently to be introduced—he was, one thought, the most dispensable member of this luncheon entourage. Then people noticed his eyes, that laser stare. Suddenly, the slightly built man became at once the sum of—yet really none of—the parts millions of moviegoers so admire him for: Travis Bickle, the psychotic killer of *Taxi Driver*, Vito Corleone, the emerging Mafia don of *Godfather II*, and Monroe Stahr, the tormented studio executive of *The Last Tycoon*. And in this briefest of instants on the Polo Lounge terrace, Robert De Niro lost again his much-cherished anonymity, as the patrons of the famous restaurant began to whisper, to shift in their chairs, in recognition of his presence. And as they reacted to him, Robert De Niro reacted to them. His actor's instinct meshing in high gear, his body tensed. A twinge of fear seemed momentarily to cross his face; his emblematic sense of privacy was stripped away. Then he caught himself, reined in his feelings, and once again stood there, being introduced, mumbling polite, monosyllabic greetings. Only his eyes suggested that beneath his painfully shy and uncomfortable surface personality lurked a screen presence so electrifying and varied that at last America may have produced an actor good enough to rank with the best; to my mind, he's already on the way to becoming an American Laurence Olivier.

Stardom of this magnitude usually affects actors in one of two ways. There's the Clark Gable Effect, in which the actor's life and off-screen persona become so large they unify all of his roles. And there's the Disappearing Talent Effect, which causes a superstar—like Barbra Streisand—to believe that celebrity is a right and any performance will please an undiscriminating public. Robert De Niro has invented a third approach: He hasn't changed at all. He remains the same ultra-private, hardworking, driven, sweet-tempered, brilliant, gentle, compulsive soul he was at the beginning of his career. His problem, if he has one, is that people who don't know him tend to take his need for privacy as aloofness. His dilemma is that as more and more people recognize his talent and fewer and fewer people are able to get to know him, his solution to the celebrity game will make him appear as haughty as Streisand and as cavalier as Gable —when the truth is that Robert De Niro has always been a loner.

And a very wary loner at that.

He doesn't talk to reporters, though he will torment

them for weeks, waiting while he makes up his mind. But if he's courteous—or perverse—enough to consider an interview, he doesn't extend that privilege to his friends: They're under strict instructions from him to defend the wall of secrecy he's thrown up around his life. They tend to cooperate. "Now that he's a star, he's in an incredible position to help us," a close friend says. "Nobody wants to jeopardize that. People are afraid of him now." Another friend recalls spending the afternoon at a party with De Niro, then describing that scene to others later that evening, after which he and De Niro were planning to go to the movies. They never got there: "De Niro blew up. He turned on me and looked at me with that stare of his and said, 'How dare you discuss these things?' and then stormed out." An actress who did allow herself to be interviewed for this profile was told by De Niro's confidante Shelley Winters that she was off De Niro's list of friends. And when I was interviewing another actor— who has been close to De Niro for years—and the telephone rang, I watched him turn from white to ashen; the caller, Robert De Niro, didn't approve of his friend's guest.

All this would make sense if his friends really had deep, dark secrets which, if revealed, might hurt De Niro. But no one does. In fact, it took many of his friends two years to learn that De Niro was living with Dihanne Abbot, the exquisite mulatto who would become his wife five years after they first met at a party in New York. The popular theory was that De Niro was trying to protect the fact that America's foremost Italian-Jewish actor was living with a black woman. Harvey Keitel, an actor who has often worked with De Niro and is one of his oldest friends, laughs about that. "Are you kidding?" Keitel says. "If you asked Bobby that, he'd say something like,

'Is Di black?'" Then Keitel catches himself and breaks the conversation off. De Niro's cult of silence brings the shield down again.

"The thing is, once you get to the bottom of Bobby, once you penetrate all that paranoia and secrecy that he surrounds himself with, you'll find out that at the bottom of Bobby is really . . . *nothing,* " an old girlfriend suspects. She's missed it a little. The reason De Niro seems like such a pale personality is because he is so completely dedicated to acting; his life takes place in front of the cameras. As Paul Shrader, author of *Taxi Driver,* says, "He doesn't feel the need to establish an identity apart from his screen persona. He doesn't want to. The only thing he desires to be public about himself is his work. That's the only thing he estimates has any real value."

From the beginning, De Niro groomed himself for the artist's reclusive life. He wasn't like the other kids in New York's Little Italy: he was half Jewish, half Italian. His mother, Virginia Admiral, abandoned an accomplished career as a painter to support her only child after her divorce. Robert De Niro was two years old when his parents separated; he was to know his father as a gifted abstract impressionist often afflicted with "painter's block." De Niro, Senior, was a friend of DeKooning and Pollock, but was denied—until recently—a shadow of their success. He was, he recalls, always the respected but little-known artist, forced to accept "teaching at four or five places at once, not making any money, a nightmare." Yet he remained an effervescent personality, who, other artists say, "makes friends easily." Robert De Niro, Junior, went the other way, perhaps because he felt trapped living with his mother and her boyfriend, Manny Farber, a painter and film critic. Farber was known for strong opinions and irascibility in those years, and De

Niro, who requires as much courtesy and devotion from his associates as he gives them, may have been relieved when Farber moved to California. Certainly he was not relieved to be reintroduced to Farber, after all these years, at a recent Hollywood party. "Do you remember me? I used to go out with your mother," Farber said. "You have unbelievable eyes. Just like your father. You're much more like your father than your mother." Robert De Niro, according to others at that party, couldn't get away fast enough.

So in Little Italy, where nicknames last for a lifetime, Robert De Niro was known as "Bobby Milk." He would stand across the street from a group of kids and watch them, but he was always so shy and thin and pale—pale as milk—that he never joined them. This near-pathological shyness kept him an outsider in Hollywood. A hostess there remembers giving a party after De Niro's overwhelming performances in *Bang the Drum Slowly* and *Mean Streets.* When the word got out that the brilliant young actor would be present, hundreds showed up. "I was looking everywhere for him," the hostess recalls. "Then somebody came in and said two bums were outside in the bushes. I went out, and it was De Niro talking to Al Pacino. He was afraid to come inside."

But the shyness made him burn to express himself, ever since, at age ten, he was the Cowardly Lion in the P.S. 41 production of *The Wizard of Oz.* By sixteen, he'd dropped out of high school and was studying with Stella Adler, appearing in any Off-Off-Broadway showcase or non-Equity production that would have him. He was a fanatic about learning his craft. "You never saw Bobby, even at that age, when he didn't have a paperback book or something under his arm," a friend says. "You'd go into his house on Fourteenth Street and there'd be a zillion hats around, all kinds of costumes." Casting director Marion Dougherty will never forget the day the young De Niro came in to see her: "He had a portfolio in which he appeared as an eighty-year-old man, and in costumes of all kinds. I had never seen anything like that."

Neither had his fellow actors at the Lee Strasberg Studio. Actress Sally Kirkland first met De Niro when he was dating her roommate; she was impressed by his habit of always bringing flowers. Kirkland thought he was merely "sweet." Then she went downtown and saw him in an Off-Off-Broadway play, *Glamor, Glory and Gold.* "He played five parts," Kirkland says. "I'd never seen anything so brilliant. I went backstage and told him: 'Do you know that you are going to be the most incredible star?' " De Niro's reaction was characteristic. "He was unbelievably shy. I thought perhaps I was embarrassing him. But I could tell that, more than anything, he wanted to believe it." After gifted performances in Brian De Palma's low-budget films *Greetings* and *Hi, Mom!*, De Niro found it was easier to make others believe in him— which turned out to be the way he entered the restrictive circle of Hollywood film actors.

It was through actress Sylvia Miles that he met Shelley Winters, who cast him in her play *One Night Stands of a Noisy Passenger.* He didn't let her down. For the fifteen-second karate bit that was part of his role, he studied karate for several months so that, night after night, he could crack a board with one blow. That kind of dedication turned Winters from a believer into what De Niro calls "my Jewish mother." She recommended De Niro next to the "King of the B's," Roger Corman, suggesting De Niro for a part as her young psychotic boyfriend in *Bloody Mama.* His first Hollywood role didn't faze De

Niro; he prepared his Arkansas twang by spending weeks in the Ozarks before shooting began. Corman was able to use him for double duty: as dialogue coach and actor. Shelley Winters had never witnessed anyone live a part like De Niro, and she was amazed by his professionalism: "The character was supposed to deteriorate physically, and Bobby got so frail we all became alarmed. His face got this horrible chalky look and his skin broke out in disgusting sores. At night, we'd all go out and stuff ourselves, and Bobby would just sit, drinking water. When he gets to the soul of a character, he refuses to let go. This is going to sound crazy, but . . . Bobby got killed in *Bloody Mama*. His part was over. He could have gone home. On the day we were to shoot the burial scene, I walked over to the open grave, looked down, and got the shock of my life. 'Bobby!' I screamed. 'I don't believe this! You get out of that grave this minute!' "

But ask De Niro about his lavish, near-obsessional preparations and his answer will be noncommittal, punctuated with much hesitation: "I really can't talk about it . . . I mean, I just never know what's going to work . . . I just do the best I can for every role . . ." It's not that he's inarticulate, but that his method is private, inward-looking, too fragile to promote on the Hollywood meat rack; he can't talk about what he does and then waste time correcting the inevitable misimpressions. One result of that distance De Niro maintains, even toward his peers, is that although he's perhaps our most versatile actor, there are increasingly few directors he can work with.

The directors who work with De Niro tend to be like De Niro himself: committed, intuitive, students of gesture rather than language. Marty Scorsese, who directed De Niro in *Mean Streets, Taxi Driver,* and *New York, New*

York, hired him the first time because "he was wearing a hat and tilted it a certain way, saying he thought the character would wear it that way." He didn't need to see De Niro act after that performance. De Niro had simply researched himself right into the part.

As the films became more prestigious, De Niro's commitment to his craft became even more passionate, until his personal life barely existed. His friend Al Pacino was responding to this when he tried to keep De Niro out of *Godfather II;* he feared he'd be overshadowed by De Niro. De Niro was certain that would be impossible; he'd spent months researching the character and come up with only indecision. Then he figured it out. As he told one of Marlon Brando's friends, "There's only one thing I can do: I have to do Brando. I have to imitate Brando rather than create a new character." Brando's friend told Brando, who commented, "I can understand why he would want to do that, but he won't be able to." When the film was released, Brando agreed with those who voted De Niro his Oscar that De Niro is "the most talented actor working today."

The approval of actors he respects and his own self-analysis seem all that count for De Niro; it's his protection against the millions whose love he perceives could smother him. So his opinion of his Oscar wasn't disingenuous or the mouthing-off of a young kid; the deceptively boyish De Niro was thirty-two when he won his Oscar in 1975. And right in character. "Lots of people who win the Oscar don't deserve it," he said then, "so it makes you a little cynical about how much it means. Did it mean much to me? Well, I don't know. It changes your life like anything like that will change your life. People react to it. I mean: It's not *bad* winning it."

For De Niro, the important *Godfather* story is not that

he overshadowed Pacino—he really didn't—but that his preparation technique worked; he'd already learned Sicilian for his role in *The Gang That Couldn't Shoot Straight,* and only had to brush up for *Godfather.* The Oscar vindicated not De Niro the personality but De Niro the actor, and he threw himself still deeper into his approach with *Taxi Driver,* for which he spent time driving a cab and hanging around the animal cages at the zoo. *The Last Tycoon* was a daring, 180-degree change for him; its preparation included a thirty-pound weight loss and residence in an oversized Beverly Hills mansion. For *New York, New York,* he learned how to play a passable jazz saxophone.

His friends say that De Niro is now almost entirely the sum of his parts, that it's impossible to see where the actor ends and the person begins. "In between pictures, Bobby doesn't exist," Shelley Winters says. "I don't know where the human being is—and even with Marlon, I know where he is." The effect of that intensity on women has been described as "Svengali-like." Former girlfriends call him "a disease that gets into your system," "a black cloud" who, though intellectual, exudes macho sexuality. In that sense, this thin, modest-looking man is a paradoxical Brando; he's an unlikely sex symbol. Yet a former girlfriend, who hadn't seen him in five years, recalls, "One night at a party, I felt someone staring at me. I looked up, and there he was across the room. I felt his eyes were drilling bullet holes into me." Another remembers that whenever she drove somewhere with De Niro, he kept his eyes on her, never the road. Like the woman he ultimately would marry, these former girlfriends are earthy, robust types, with unending warmth, quite different from descriptions of his own mother. His appeal to them was his little-boy sweetness and macho sensuality, or, as one simply says, "his eyes," as if that explains everything.

De Niro's wedding was the perfect example of how those eyes are focused—on his career. In June, 1976, as his friends gathered for the ceremony at New York's Ethical Culture Society, almost everyone was a show-business professional from one or another of De Niro's films. Sam Spiegel and Elia Kazan represented *The Last Tycoon.* John Hancock, who directed De Niro in *Bang the Drum Slowly,* was there with his actress-wife, Dorothy Tristan. Shelley Winters, Julie Bovasso, and Joe Papp came from De Niro's apprenticeship period, as did *Time* film critic Jay Cocks and his wife, actress Verna Fields. Sally Kirkland, Barry Primus, and Harvey Keitel made up a contingent of old friends, and Marty Scorsese was his fellow graduate of New York's Little Italy. "Everybody there," Paul Shrader recalls, "was somebody who had helped Bobby to become a different person." Somebody better? "Absolutely not," Shrader says. "Somebody different."

Marriage has hardly made De Niro more outgoing, although it has given Dihanne a higher profile. There will be no accusations that she's riding her husband's career, though; in her brief role in *Welcome to L.A.* she gives an inarguably professional performance. Privately, she has borne her husband his first child, Rafael, named after the hotel in Rome where he was conceived. De Niro, already the stepfather of Dihanne's eight-year-old daughter from her previous marriage, threw himself into parenthood as if it were the biggest part of his life. He'd already given up the $70-a-month walk-up on Four-teenth Street where Manny Farber and Virginia Admiral used to live for a townhouse on St. Luke's Place. Now he's building a Los Angeles home for his family in quiet Brentwood. "He's a very simple person who takes care of his family," a friend says, referring to the aunts and uncles who always seem to be visiting the De Niros these days. "And to see him with Rafe is just unbelievable."

Apparently family life gratifies De Niro as much as the movies do. After working back-to-back in Bernardo Bertolucci's five-hour *1900, The Last Tycoon,* and *New York, New York,* he's decided to take a year off to be with his wife and child. But in a time when stars take sabbaticals and never return, there's no reason to worry about Robert De Niro. He's already preparing for his next picture, about 1940s heavyweight boxer Jake LaMotta; by the time shooting begins, he expects to be an accomplished fighter and weigh in at two hundred pounds. Don't expect boxing to work miracles on De Niro's personality, transforming him into a self-confident extrovert. LaMotta is one more character in the mosaic of Robert De Niro's larger-than-life persona. As for his lust for privacy, De Niro knew all along how that would resolve itself. Before *Mean Streets* was released, a friend took him aside and asked, "You're so paranoid now, Bobby. How are you going to be when you're a star?"

"Worse," Robert De Niro said.

MARTHE KELLER

arthe Keller, impossibly tall and swathed in flowing white chiffon that made her look even taller, even more Nordic, stepped out of the hired limousine followed by an unimaginably short and chunky man. He was John Schlesinger, director of *Midnight Cowboy, Day of the Locust,* and, this year, *Marathon Man,* in which Marthe Keller made her Hollywood debut. Because this is New York, where audiences are more inclined to applaud the director than the star, the actress approached the cameras NBC had brought to Columbus Circle for *The Big Event* without being recognized. This night the applause would be all for Schlesinger.

All evening long the crowd had been growing, rattling the windows of the Gulf + Western skyscraper with cheers for hometown favorites Dustin Hoffman and Sylvia Miles. The ovations built weirdly as each star walked a hundred-odd yards on fuchsia carpeting for the waiting millions; there was a rippling of applause from the people in front, a buzzing as the names of the stars —Petula Clark, Polly Bergen, Anjelica Huston, Lauren Hutton—were passed back through the crowd to the latecomers, then a full-fledged *Day of the Locust* scream just as the bewildered star reached the revolving door and disappeared. As it happened, Schlesinger and Keller got separated by interviewers, and Marthe Keller had to walk the last thirty yards with only a halfhearted smattering of applause for company. The elegant former ballerina remained unperturbed. She could afford to. On Columbus Circle few may have known who she was, but in a few months she would be appearing everywhere as one of Hollywood's newest faces.

She would, at the very least, be appearing at Elaine's Restaurant, on New York's upper East Side. One night, a few months later, the elegant Keller will stride through the room. Heads will turn and finally, the star of the just-released *Black Sunday* will be recognized. But this night, Keller will ignore everyone in her haste to creep up on a back table—its occupants are Elaine's only diners who will not have seen her arrive. Keller will wink at the maître d', motion for him to keep quiet, then suddenly she'll pounce—kissing the back of the head of a petite dark-headed man sitting at that rear table. Al Pacino will turn around and laugh. A moment later, Keller will be sitting on his lap. Since the filming of *Bobby Deerfield*—a love story starring Keller and Pacino—in the summer of 1976, the small, glum Method actor and the tall, sunny, Swiss-German actress have hardly been apart. By the following spring they were living together, just a few blocks from Elaine's. Inevitably, somebody at the table asks the Swiss-German emigrée how long she is planning to stay in New York. She hesitates, then winks at Pacino. "Forever, I hope," is Keller's reply.

It's not exactly your everyday 1970s Cinderella story —dancer turns actress—but it has nonetheless a fairy-tale quality. It begins in a screening room, with Paramount producer Robert Evans watching *And Now My Love,* Claude Lelouch's love story in which Keller gives a tour-de-force performance as a girl who ages from sixteen to sixty. The actress is unknown to Evans, but he is moved to tears by this modern Garbo, remote yet vulnerable. He auditions her for *Marathon Man*—Dustin Hoffman won't play love scenes with women whose "chemistry" is bad—and even though director Schlesinger had no affection for *And Now My Love,* Keller wins the part. In short order, she adds *Black Sunday* (with Bruce Dern) and *Bobby Deerfield* (with Al Pacino) to her credits. "It's the most amazing thing," a proud Evans says of his newest prodigy. "Here's a girl who a year ago didn't speak one word of English and has now starred in three big pictures opposite top leading men—and they say there are no parts for women around!"

But Bob Evans's hottest discovery since Ali MacGraw cannot possibly be the woman who answers the door of Marthe Keller's apartment on Paris's Left Bank. This Marthe Keller—towering, raw-boned, a navy-blue-and-white kerchief wrapped around her head, her lack of make-up accentuating candy-drop eyes, a plain Nordic mouth and nose, and a purple scar the size of a baby's hand on her forehead—looks so little like the beauty of both *And Now My Love* and *Marathon Man* that she has to laugh when I ask, "Is Marthe Keller here?" Because this Marthe Keller looks . . . exhausted. The beginnings of purple hollows circle her eyes. All day she has been in a dubbing session with John Frankenheimer, helping him put the final touches on *Black Sunday.* She is squeezing the American reporter into her free hours; then Mickey Knox, her dialogue coach, will arrive for more arduous work, the refining of Keller's accent into American syntax for her role opposite Pacino. She will be ready for Mickey Knox—the ultra-disciplined Swiss-born and German-language-educated twenty-nine-year-old has decorated her plant-filled living room with lists of words ("upholstery," "prevaricate," "sociology") that she still mispronounces.

If Marthe Keller looks tired, there are reasons: "This is my sixth movie in thirteen months. I did tests for *Marathon Man,* then I came back to do three French films in a row; the last one, *La Gipia,* I finished on a Saturday night. On Sunday, I flew over to start *Marathon Man.* Then I flew to Miami for *Black Sunday.* I finished that and immediately flew to Paris to start rehearsing *Bobby Deerfield* the next morning." Clearly, Keller is overworked, driven. "She's unbelievably ambitious," says an American friend, "and so far Marthe hasn't made any mistakes."

So Marthe Keller, purple circles and all, is not complaining this afternoon as she sits in her duplex, as neatly arranged as the nearby Luxembourg Gardens. Instead, she is leaning forward on one love seat, her face bundled into its handkerchief, washerwoman plain, concerned with the moment. At this moment, she is concerned with making a member of the American press feel comfortable. "Are you sure you don't want anything?" she asks me in a German-French-accented English. "Only a mineral water? Some coffee? How about some wine? Some cheese? Come here and look at the garden! Are you sure I can't get you . . . anything??" You would think she is playing the insecure, overanxious mother role till you remember that Keller is still learning conversational English and using interviews as a high-pressure language lab. For Keller—who some have called snobbish and glacial—these questions are a foreigner's way of making contact in a language in which she still does not feel utterly at home. So she tries especially hard to make a good impression, harder than an American actress might. The phone has to ring only once for her to leave it off the hook, apologizing profusely for taking the two-minute phone call. Still, you can't help wondering if Keller's graciousness will remain when the I'm-a-new-star glitter wears off, when the novelty of being interviewed by the American press turns from fun to compulsion. For now, at least, she is at her peak, our very newest Bergmanesque import, close in both manner and appearance to actress Bibi Andersson, who, by coincidence, turns out to be Keller's closest friend.

This intense serio-Nordic sense of self which seems the common denominator linking Liv Ullmann, Bibi Andersson, and Marthe Keller is very different from the romantic persona Keller projected in *And Now My Love*. In that frothy fantasy, she whipped her way through a multigenerational love story as the spoiled, intelligent, but very beautiful heiress who sets off to find herself. Along the way she falls in love with singer Gilbert Becaud, is taken on an around-the-world please-forget-him trip by her shoe-magnate father, only to find temporary sympathy from a series of miscast lovers until—finally— she meets the man of her dreams: an ex-convict film director bound for New York. Could Keller—who so convincingly plays coldblooded killers in both *Marathon Man* and *Black Sunday* that her mere presence causes an audience's knuckles to whiten—share any real-life romantic qualities with the heroine of *And Now My Love*? It seems an innocent question, but Keller fidgets slightly. "Well, yes," she says slowly in an even-softer French patois, "it's my story and Claude Lelouch's story . . ." She pauses. "I mean, it's not exactly our story. He wasn't in prison and I wasn't a rich girl, but most everything else is the same. We were both in Dallas at the French week given by that store . . . you know, the Neiman-Marcus?

Marie Brenner

And Lelouch and I had a film that was shown and so I had to be there and so did he . . ." She takes a breath; then her words tumble out even faster. "So we left together, we didn't know each other before . . . I mean, I knew *about* him, who he was, he'd seen me in the movies, but—can you believe it?—we'd never met. So you know how it is when two people meet each other and have the same taste and like the same things?" Her voice trails off, as it will through the afternoon when she is clearly not pleased with any personal interrogation. Her gaze rests on one of the dozens of photographs of her son. From the close-ups of the boy cavorting with his mother or smiling into the camera, all curly-haired and button-eyed, he looks too old to have been a product of her three-year relationship with Lelouch. One had heard that five-year-old Alexandre was fathered by director Philippe de Broca *(King of Hearts, That Man from Rio)*— did Keller divorce de Broca for Lelouch after their fateful meeting on a 747? Nordic reserve prevents her expression from even flickering. "De Broca and I were never married," she says evenly. She is ready to move on to the next topic.

Which is, of course, her new career as an American actress and possible superstar, the result of her role in *Marathon Man*—a part she almost didn't get. Her version of this story has less to do with Schlesinger's dislike of her performance in *And Now My Love* than it does with Marthe Keller's cavalier approach to her Hollywood screen test. "We had dinner together the night before and everything was perfect and then I went back to the hotel and suddenly I got so nervous that I asked for a whole bottle of red wine because I couldn't sleep. At eight in the morning, somebody rings the phone and I answer in French or German." She stops to take a gulp of air. Suddenly, her face is full of life, its former reserve gone. "Only when I realize that I don't know where I am, I look down. And an empty bottle of red wine is crooked in my arm . . . I was completely drunk! I had never been like that in my life! So my agent came to pick me up and bring me some coffee, and I was *laaafffing* like crazy—so they think I had a sense of humor, you know? And I saw people like Dustin Hoffman and Roy Scheider, like Laurence Olivier, and I was yelling, 'Hi! Nice to meet you!' Because I didn't care. I couldn't talk English! I was improvising in French, Italian, in German. I saw the rushes later . . . I look like Frankenstein!" But yet she passed Schlesinger's test, and did so well in *Marathon Man* that she was asked to play a terrorist again in *Black Sunday;* this time she's a PLO member conspiring to blow up the Super Bowl. Amazingly enough, at first Keller refused the role. "For political reasons. But after I talk with a few intelligent people they tell me I am crazy. And the more I keep refusing, the more they want me. It's like being in love! So now I'm very happy I did it because it's a beautiful movie, like a documentary."

And repressing her left-wing rhetoric and tendencies (Keller took part in the '68 Paris uprising), agreeing to star in *Black Sunday,* led her to *Bobby Deerfield.* There is a special warmth in her eyes when she talks about this latest role. "For me, this is the best part I ever have. Because the two other parts, they are action. Thrillers. And this woman in *Bobby Deerfield* is a real woman, and she is dying. It's a movie about relationships, feelings, sentiments, love and death; it's very deep and very sad. I fall in love with Al Pacino, who is a race-car driver, and in the film the part I play is that of a woman who eats too much, smokes too much, talks too much; I ask ten questions when I could ask one, and he takes an hour to answer! Everything is so crazy about us! And when these two people meet each other, there's a whole world." Off-screen as well; in Paris, all summer, people connected with *Bobby Deerfield* spoke of the growing romance between Pacino and Keller, who could be seen drinking wine together after a long day's shooting. And Keller's relationship with Lelouch *did* end almost two years before. On these subjects the normally voluble Marthe Keller is again silent. But nobody else is. "Marthe and Al are having a thing," director Sydney Pollack told several friends in Paris that summer. Columns had her linked not only to Pacino, but also to Bob Evans, her *Marathon Man* producer. "Marthe and I?" Evans laughs, before the Keller-Pacino romance was public news. "I've never even taken her to lunch! Besides, I hear she's with Al."

It's not surprising that Marthe seems relieved to talk about her childhood in Bascl, hcr father, now a retired jockey, and his relationship with her mother. "They are so beautiful, the two of them. They never argue. That is why I never marry, because I can't find anyone who is like my father. I would love to be like them! Can you believe they never have anyone else in their life? It is so *bee-yoo-tee-full!*" They encouraged her childhood studies in dance and endorsed the theater after a skiing accident forced her to switch professions. When Keller was eighteen, she won a fellowship to a Munich theater; within a few years she had acted "in everything from Pinter to Shakespeare to Moliere to everything."

But all that training hardly prepared the twenty-year-old actress for the summons from a famous Hollywood producer. He'd seen her picture and wanted to test her for a possible studio contract. Keller is completely relaxed now, standing in her tiled country-style kitchen boiling water for tea. "It was *awe-ful.* I was shown in to see this man and I was so young, so naive. I was a *baby*. I didn't know anything. And this producer is looking at my pictures and getting very excited, and he said to me, 'Would you like to make love with another woman, because if you would, I would like to watch. And I'm going to give you a five-year contract.' I just look at him because I don't know what this means. Then he said to me, 'Well, if you're not a lesbian, then what about letting me watch you with a man?' So I keep looking at him, and then I begin to understand—I burst into tears and start crying, crying. Then I call him a son of a bitch in German and then I run out, but it showed me that I was not yet ready to become a film actress. And this is the way I thought it was in the movies, with the big producers. So I am grateful to the big Hollywood producer. Because of him, I went back to Munich, to the theater, for another five years, and I became a well-known actress on the German stage."

Enter director Philippe de Broca, who called her to Paris to test for an ingenue role. Keller won the part *and* the filmmaker, then almost didn't stay to make the film. The memory makes her smile. "When I arrived in Paris, it was May of 1968, and the whole place was in revolution, so the movie was pushed back. I didn't know what to do—I had to go back to Berlin because my theater vacation was over—but I didn't want to leave until I'd finished the film. So I debated with myself, should I stay or go back? *So* . . ." She grins. "I decided . . . Berlin was . . . *far.*"

Since that film, Marthe Keller has appeared in dozens of French movies and has starred in her own television series, *Les Demoiselles d'Avignon* (a Frenchified *Roman Holiday*), but it wasn't until she was seen nightly on French TV that Marthe Keller's name became a household word in her adopted country. "It was so funny," she recalls, *"Demoiselles d'Avignon* premiered on television the night my son was born. I went into the American Hospital in Paris to give birth, and nobody knew me. Not one person said hello. When I left, all the nurses gathered around and asked for my autograph."

By the time Alexandre was born, Keller's relationship with his father was long over. Was she worried about supporting her son? Without hesitating she answers, "Absolutely not. I came into this apartment—and I didn't have one cent. And this apartment costs a *fortune*. So I said, 'What am I going to do?' Then I decided. I asked everybody to give me some money. And it was crazy! So now that I have money, I buy . . . *nothing*. You see how I am dressed. I no longer have a need."

And she doesn't. Sitting in that kitchen, wearing sloppy white denims and a long cotton top, Marthe Keller radiates, if not self-confidence, at least tremendous self-acceptance. She does not feel compelled to dwell on her status with de Broca or on the problems of bringing up a child without a full-time father. She and de Broca, she says, are still "best friends." De Broca and Alexandre have "a beautiful relationship." As she explains it, she makes me want to believe her: "De Broca and I were separated when Alexandre was born, so he never felt the loss." Seeing the Swiss I'd-rather-not-discuss-it look return to Keller's eyes, I stop myself from asking how *she* felt when she was giving birth, knowing her child's father had long since gone away. Instead I ask, how did her parents react when she announced she was pregnant? This brings a laugh. "Oh! My mother fell-down-black." Her voice travels up and down a full octave. "But, you know, I did the whole thing before I told her—I invited her to the mountains where I have a house, and I waited for the right sunset. We were outside, the cows were around, bells were ringing, the sun was going down . . . and I said, 'I think I should tell you something: I'm pregnant.' And I couldn't finish because my mother had already fainted. But before she fell, she said, 'And you're not married?' So I had to lie and say we were getting married, even though it was already over between De Broca and me . . .'' Keller's face, pained by these memories, suddenly lightens again. "Oh, today, she has such a *big* laugh, my mother does, when she thinks about how silly she was! But my father—he was *always* thrilled. He just said, 'I'm so glad to have a grandson.' "

Indeed, besides Pacino, Alexandre is *the* man in his mother's life. When Marthe Keller speaks of him, she's no longer the serious Liv Ullmann–like actress, but a proud mother, dragging down picture after picture of her son to illustrate the point. "My Alexandre, he is so *tender,*" she says, stretching that word until it's at least four syllables. "Let me tell you a beautiful story. He was just on holiday with his father and his father said to him, 'Here's a little country store, I want to give you five francs, go and buy whatever you like; they have little cars, shoes, candies, cheese.' They had *everything,* and his father waited outside for him, and he came out a few minutes later and handed his father four francs, fifty, and his father said to him, 'What did you buy?' And Alexandre said, 'A postcard for my mama and a stamp. I want to write her a letter.' I just got the postcard, and I was crying, it was so beautiful."

This is not the kind of anecdote most stars would whip out for the American press; you believe Marthe Keller when she talks about her son and their special times in her mountain retreat in Verbier, Switzerland. You believe Marthe Keller even when she talks about retiring to that mountaintop in Verbier, where life is simpler. A special intensity underlies her words. Yes, she's had her first taste of the star's life in America, but she's also had her first taste of the very real dangers that can be involved. Recently, a Los Angeles crazy tried to murder both Keller and her son. "During the shooting of *Marathon Man,* Alexandre and I were home alone and somebody rang the bell and said, 'Marthe Keller?' and I opened the door and there was this little woman, about thirty-five, very strange, and she said to me, 'Are *you* Marthe Keller?' and I guess she was very disappointed because here I was without the make-up and she expected me to be the way I look in my photographs. And she was so strange that I closed the door. She had her foot in, so I pushed her out. Then I noticed the gun. And I asked her on the intercom what she wanted. She said, 'I don't want nothing. Just to kill you. You and your son within twenty-four hours . . .' And she was serious. The woman came back with a gun three times and the guard of my neighborhood wouldn't let her in. So the police said, 'How can we arrest her if she hasn't killed you?' I stayed up all night and Alexandre said, 'Who is that woman, Mommy?' and I said, 'Nobody, just a bad woman,' and then he said, 'Wait a minute.' And Alexandre went to his room" —for the first time in this story, Marthe begins to smile—"and he came back with a water pistol and said, 'Don't be afraid, Mama, you sleep with *me* tonight.' Finally they caught the woman and sent her to a mental hospital. The psychiatrist released her after twenty minutes and she came back again. The next day they moved me into Bel-Air, and I lived like a real movie star with a bodyguard the rest of the time I was in California." So it's no surprise that Marthe Keller would *never* live in California. "New York, yes, but Los Angeles is

. . . crazy. I guess they thought they have so many insane people out there, this one was probably harmless. Only this one came with a gun."

Telling that story in a duplex apartment high above the St. Germain, Marthe Keller seems relaxed and philosophical. The Los Angeles incident, she reminds you, was not her first close look at death. That purple scar on her forehead? A near-fatal car accident from a time when she and De Broca were living together and Alexandre was not even an idea. Keller went through the windshield —twice. "The last thing I heard someone say was 'Is she dead?' And when I woke up in the hospital, I was covered with plaster from head to toe. That was the only time I was really scared. I thought I would never be able to act again." Fortunately, Marthe Keller was wrong. But why keep the scar when it could be so easily removed? "Why bother to have it fixed?" She shrugs, unashamed to wear her history.

A few minutes later, she is talking about Al Pacino again—Pacino the actor, that is. "He is the most honest person in the world. And if he can't do some bit of business, he won't fake it." My eye takes in the scene: the living room furnished only with essentials, the pictures of young Alexandre strewn across the couch, the actress-mother speaking intently to an unknown American, never looking at the tape recorder or the clock. She is still searching for the perfect description of Al Pacino. "He's just so *honest!*" Marthe Keller exclaims. And so is she.

THE VICE-PRESIDENT OF CREATIVE AFFAIRS (Near-to-Life Hollywood Fiction)

The Vice-President of Creative Affairs is thinly disguised fiction for purely technical reasons: The experience of the dozen female executives in Hollywood is so fundamentally similar that it seemed senseless to single any one of them out. The deal I describe here wasn't lost to the woman at, say Universal, for example; it's been lost, at various times, by a woman at each studio—and the women in the agencies as well. If I've taken liberties with the facts, it's in the inclusion of a romance between the executive and a male writer; the social isolation in Los Angeles is so acute and the demands of a studio job are so great that it's hard for a woman—for anyone, in fact—to be successful in both her personal and professional life.

The first call of the morning was not going well. "Just tell me one thing," the vice-president of creative affairs finally snapped when the man on the other end had finished welshing on his commitment. "Are you happy that this deal's blown? Are you *happy* that every single time I'm ready to put one of your clients in development you suddenly start talking five months instead of six weeks for a viable first draft when you know very well that those goddamn writers are going out on strike? Are you happy that, thanks to you and your client, we won't be able to do the Melvin Dummar story?"

Somewhere in the hills above Sunset, in a house with a terrific view of billboards, steel telephone poles, and the flats of Hollywood, the Hollywood agent agreed that the loss of the Melvin Dummar story would rob the moviegoing audience of a great movie and cost the vice-president's studio an easy $15 million profit. But his client was not to blame.

The vice-president persisted. "Yes. I know your client came to me with twelve ideas and the Dummar story wasn't one of them. But he seemed to really get into it . . ." She paused. "All right, so he did mention that he wanted to do that other thing more, but how was I supposed to know that Fox would give him a commitment, just like that? *I* wanted to ram both of them through, *I* wanted one to ride the other, *I* wanted to give him a two-picture deal . . ." A moment passed. "*I* couldn't have told you that. *I* couldn't have told you that. We—at the very least—should have been offered matching rights . . . Does your client know how this studio's been used?"

She leaned back in her Breuer chair and stared into the bright sunlight outside. It still looked like siesta time out on the lot where forty years earlier men had made pictures, not just deals. There had been stars then, too, more stars than you could find in the Los Angeles skies these nights. Now there were six, maybe even only five who were bankable; she wasn't sure. All that she was sure of was that most major studios were barely releasing a dozen films a year. And that was in a good year, a year like the one UA was having and her studio wasn't. Well, she shouldn't complain. At least things weren't so bad at her studio that she couldn't make deals, which was, though they denied it, what she'd heard was going on at another studio across town. Which was why she had invested a month of care in the Melvin Dummar story—as soon as she heard that Warren Beatty's Howard Hughes project was floundering, she knew she had a wedge with this agent's screenwriter. And then, after all her foreplay, he decided he liked the stroking at Fox better. She sighed. This wouldn't be the first deal she had nurtured along only to see it wind up on another studio's development list. Anyway, it wouldn't be good business to let him think she was all that upset.

"Well . . . Maybe I could have been crazier for his idea. But, let's stay calm, okay? We're all going to be in this business a long time. After all, we're a tight little family, aren't we? Of course we'll do business again."

But not so soon, she thought, *not if I can help it.* In New York there would have been general agreement that this agent had seriously misbehaved, using her offer as if it were a strategy point. Well, she wouldn't stand for it. She'd teach him how many buyers there remained in this town, she'd . . . do nothing of the kind. Who was she kidding? She knew agents had the power. It seemed like a previous incarnation, not just a short two years ago, when she'd been an agent, that she'd felt that same power herself: that thrill of controlling a half-decent screenplay and watching the studios fall over themselves pitching deals for half a million up front and 10 percent of the gross in the back end. At those prices, it always seemed paradoxical that it didn't make any difference to anybody's career if the end result bombed. The film wouldn't be out for three years, and by then every man or woman involved in its conception would be working somewhere else, taking credit only for the box-office winners. She called this the Mayflower Syndrome. You could fill Schwab's with the number of Paramount alumni who claimed to have developed *The Godfather.*

Dealing with agents often tired her, made her feel she was condemned to conversations like Möbius strips: endless, twisted, going nowhere. But this call, though disappointing, was a stimulant, really a rehearsal for her morning ahead. Why? Because this morning she'd be playing both creative executive and agent; if her stratagem worked, she'd earn her $45,000 yearly salary at one meeting, with her new project alone. To hell with the Melvin Dummar story. At last she had a script she believed in. In fact, she'd been "plumping the pillows" on *Freefall* for weeks. Now it just needed a little more push, maybe some last-minute corridor politicking. Whom should she collar?

She paced her office, reviewing the corporate cast and fashioning an approach for each of the other five members of the "creative group." On her desk lay the typed call sheet with its thirty names and messages. And a stack of opened mail. And a note reminding her she was meeting a New York publishing lady at La Scala for the ritual twelve-thirty lunch. Ordinarily these messages and obligations grabbed her, revving her system so high that many weekends she just slept, but today she ignored even the antique wicker furniture and lacquered Parson's table that soothed her as much as the Mercedes 450 SL she'd won after six months of fighting with the business-affairs people. She could see the baby-blue car in its space right outside, which was another victory, really a triumph. For five months those business-affairs people had assigned the hard-won Mercedes to a space in Siberia. So, she had merely sat back and waited for the moment when she could offer the chairman of the board a ride home. He hadn't appreciated the half-mile walk;

Mike Nichols's name had soon been painted out on the slot in front of her office and her name had been painted in.

Small triumphs augured bigger ones. Maybe she could ram *Freefall* through the morning meeting. She abandoned the idea of the personal appeal—she didn't want anyone to think of her as an irrational female—and decided instead to time her presentation like a pro, withholding her trump until she was sure she needed it.

Anyway, no one would be in yet but her and the Boy Wonder, and he didn't count; the twenty-eight-year-old Duddy Kravitz had been at his desk reading scripts since seven. He'd stay there until midnight. Sometimes she worried that his obsessiveness made her, by contrast, appear to be slacking off, when the truth was that she worked harder and longer than any of her male colleagues, even though she didn't need to, even though she was well aware of the Hollywood bottom line: Productivity had nothing to do with getting ahead. The ground rules were unwritten and Byzantine. Being seen counted. Seeming bright or clever, no matter how illusory those qualities were, was what mattered. Movement was upward or lateral—there really wasn't much difference—whether you were competent, inspired, or just so-so. The proof was everywhere; there were at least a dozen male executives around town who had been fired for losing millions, only to be hired instantly—for more money!—by their former competitors.

She had wanted to let the Boy Wonder in on the secret last night. "Leaving already?" he'd asked as she stood in his doorway at seven o'clock. "I've got so much to do, I'll probably be here till one!" She'd wondered if he was trying to make her paranoid, and, not sure that he hadn't been, she'd attacked. "When you're older, maybe you'll learn how to organize," she snapped. If anybody had ever said that to her, she might have been devastated. "This job, meeting these people, making movies," he'd confided a few moments later, "is all I've ever wanted from life."

And she'd felt a twinge, because she loved movies and she wanted this to be more than a job as well, but there was no way that an unattached thirty-six-year-old vice-president could function with so much innocence. She'd come to like the occasional evenings with Warren and Jack and Candy. She'd come to like the curling up on private screening-room couches with brandy and Krön chocolates, pretending to puff on $200-an-ounce Hawaiian grass. Yes, she liked those perks of the movie executive's life, but she knew that somewhere else life came in a larger frame, big enough to hold a man and a family and non-business friends. Few women who did what she did had all that. Compared to most of the women she knew in the industry, she was ahead of the game; she'd accepted the asexual rhythm of the moviemaker's life, this gambler's syndrome of lessened sexual energies. She was no longer shocked at her weeks of dinners with lady agents and gay men. No "real" man who did business with her would ever risk a deal by coming on.

She thought of calling her best friend now—a woman who wasn't in "the business"—to rehearse her speech, but mostly to feel a little support. She reached for the phone and dialed half the number (she was enough of a feminist not to ask her secretary to place her personal calls) and then hung up. Men played the game as teammates—women were parceled out, one to a studio. Her aloneness was supposed to be the source of some mythic strength. The operative word used to describe these female oracles was *intuitive.* So intuitively she reached for the phone again and buzzed her secretary. "Get me, in no particular order, Julia Phillips, Tom Pollock, and Ross Claiborne at Delacorte in New York."

"Ten minutes to the production meeting," her secretary said. "Do you want me to hold those until later?"

"Just try Ross Claiborne. He'll be out to lunch. Leave a message." She had learned that trick from her lawyer —calling New York when all the editors and publishers were safely at Le Madrigal. Sometimes it could take a week to connect.

Ten minutes. She didn't know how to meditate. She'd never felt—like so many of the male vice-presidents— that est had anything to teach her about improving her life. For lack of a spiritual discipline, she stared out the window. Three Indians were riding down a back street on a jeep, passing an old messenger on a dilapidated bike. She saw them as a description in a script. She took a breath, frightened suddenly at the way her mind kept taking her back to another script and its author, the man who had written *Freefall.*

She wondered if anyone had noticed, or if they assumed she was such a professional by now that everything she did was business. It had been a risk taking the author of *Freefall* to last week's buffet supper at the Directors Guild. "I want you to be seen," she'd told him, when what she really meant was: I want to be seen with you. Maybe he was that rarest of rare Hollywood writers: too shy to reach out for deals. "This will help *Freefall,*" she'd argued when he balked at parading himself in front of the Hollywood brass that would be assembled at the DGA screening.

But he'd surprised her that night. He'd waited until they'd passed the Overland exit on the Santa Monica Freeway, waited until it would be too late for her to ask him to turn around, to not take her out to his place at the beach, waited until she'd rearranged her cream-colored Alan Austin blazer with its matching pleated skirt, while she'd run her fingers through her close-cropped dark hair and frowned in her compact mirror at the abundance of premature furrows that seemed to grow deeper each day. Then finally, when she was as high from the glare of the Pacific Coast Highway lights as she was from the white wine, he'd started in on her: "Do you realize the whole night, all you were doing was talking deals? Don't you ever get sick of this? Don't you ever turn off?"

She closed her eyes, trying for the first time all night to do just that. With difficulty, she stopped herself from pointing out that he'd wasted no time glad-handing Barry Diller and introducing himself to John Calley. You couldn't tell these self-described "New York screenwriters" anything; they still believed, like Pauline Kael, that the studios were in business to make "art." *How many deals could Kael make for you?* she wanted to ask. And: *Don't you know that a film like* Freefall *will make the money that will allow us to be able to afford Bergman and Fellini?* She had wanted to say that, had wanted to scream at him that in Hollywood, movies like *Network* and *Taxi Driver* were considered art but he'd better believe the people behind both those films knew how to hustle. She had even wanted to quote to him the words of one very successful Hollywood hack: "The only way to get it on here is to go out and sell yourself. In a town where nobody reads, you have to."

Which wasn't exactly true. She read. Women read; that's why the men tended to call them the "literary ladies." It was also why, at this rate, no woman would ever run a studio. Yes, the literary ladies had made progress—after all, five years ago no female had ever been at the vice-presidential level—but still, at the critical moment in any negotiating session, some male lawyer or agent would invariably say, "You're way too pretty to be worrying about figures." Reading was what women did.

But now, as she settled herself at the elliptically shaped mahogany table with the five other members of the "creative group," she knew that the figures were *Freefall*'s strong point—once you accepted the screenwriter's intractable demand for $250,000 and 5 percent from first dollar. Would they believe that?

The head of production was droning on about a black director whose picture was being flushed into second-run houses. He wasn't taking it well, and the production chief wanted suggestions: Maybe if they found Mr. Black Power a new project, they could abort his rather-too-public discussion of Hollywood racism. The vice-president of creative affairs thought instead about a story she'd heard about the head of production and one of the blondes in their momentarily popular female sitcom. But doing it in her Jacuzzi? The smarminess of the image cheered her; at least he was human at some level. Life couldn't be all figuring out how to recoup *pari passu.*

Or could it? If the head of production wanted to get a new woman in the creative wing, he wouldn't hesitate to use her relationship with the *Freefall* screenwriter as the wedge to get her out. And that would be the end for her, unless her screenwriter became the next Bob Towne; then her position would become intractable—and probably lead to her becoming the first female head of production. But she was fantasizing. No way was her screenwriter as gifted as Bob Towne. The reality remained: Only men got fired and went to other studios; women went back to being agents. Far from depressing her, the thought was powerfully consoling. At least in the agency she'd been involved with everything, not isolated in production. And when she was an agent she'd been invited everywhere, because her host would invariably think that having her present was equivalent—in business terms—to having Carol or Paul or Lorenzo or Joanna there. That had been power. Here at the studio, nobody but the president and the chairman of the board could make the deals, so they were the only representatives at the A parties. The lines of power were not difficult to comprehend, once you knew what to look for.

"Shall we talk about *Freefall?*" the production head asked suddenly, jolting her back into the meeting room. "What does everybody think?"

The male vice-president of creative affairs—inexplicably, he made $15,000 a year more than she did—spoke first. "The script is okay. Maybe a little better than that." He spread his hands and exhibited his palms for the other executives as if the answer was plain for all to see. "But no way will we be able to get Diana Ross, and unless we have her there's no picture. You can't hand six million to Cicely Tyson or Pam Grier."

The Boy Wonder nodded vigorously in agreement, then said he had a few reservations about the basic material.

She did not say a word.

The head of production liked the writing but had more than a few reservations about the concept. He was sick of black projects. Did the world really need a film about a black balloonist at the turn of the century, even if it was Diana Ross who was floating through the stratosphere? And what about Shirley MacLaine's Amelia Earhart project? And now that *Nickelodeon* was bombing— He stopped himself. I'm not putting down Bogdanovich, the head of production said, *I* liked the picture, but we're dealing with the idea of period pieces. Costumes. Every time you shoot a train you're looking at $75,000. He hesitated. Maybe if there was a firm commitment from a bankable element . . .

She watched and waited.

The West Coast story editor said he'd heard Warner's already had a project about a black balloonist and that, unlike *Freefall,* it was a comedy. Richard Pryor was thinking about starring in it—if Mike Nichols would direct.

They turned like a wave and looked at her, waiting for her response. The moment called for a cigarette.

"I've got a commitment from Diana Ross," she said. "Diana loves the project, and Berry Gordy said if we're interested, count him in."

Which ruptured all decorum. The meeting ended on a terrific high, and she emerged victorious. Sort of. For once, she wasn't infuriated when the head of production took her triumph for himself, saying, "If Motown is really interested, I'll take over from here."

But her anger grew as she pulled out of Mike Nichols's old space and pointed the Mercedes toward Beverly Hills. She must calm herself; half a victory was better than an outright defeat. And it would be a wonderful moment telling her screenwriter that, thanks to her, he had a career. She turned on the radio and let KCLA's Erich Korngold overtures and the final shreds of "La Valse" flood the car. The leather upholstery was still new enough to tickle her nose with its musky smell, the smell of money. She leaned back in her seat, content.

But as she drove down Melrose, she felt herself tightening, her lower back cramping, her jaw aching with tension. And then it hit her: She was passing Ma Maison on the third Tuesday of the month: WOMPI day.

Women in the Motion Picture Industry had lasted a

year. "If all the men in the business play poker and tennis together," the organizers announced, "why can't the women get together and have . . . lunch." The vice-president of creative affairs had thought—they'd all thought—why not indeed? The New York media-publishing world was tight; it was time for that closeness to spread to the other sea. She had looked forward to a monthly gossip-cum-work-talk lunch with quasi-feminist overtones.

What she wasn't expecting was WOMPI—talk about clothes and men and weddings to the total exclusion of anything remotely connected to career. Well, she had thought—they'd all thought—there's more work to be done here than any of us imagined, opening up all these necessarily defensive ladies to their feelings. But then she'd brought a New York friend, a New York book editor, to a luncheon and had her eyes opened for good. The lunch turned out to be a surprise bridal shower: At thirty-five, another vice-president was donning the veil for the very first time. To celebrate, the women had thoughtfully come prepared to reveal their secrets—recipes for *crème brûlée* and *pot au feu* were attached to a rolling pin. The editor only had to look at her friend to say everything. WOMPI faded soon after that, which was lucky for the vice-president of creative affairs; she could call an agent and shoot down a deal, but she did not, for the life of her, know how she could gracefully absent herself from the hostile subcurrent at WOMPI.

She was distracted throughout lunch; the editor's "secret" list of hot books for the coming fall might as well have been physics texts, such was her haste to get back to the studio and be done with the day's business. It was silly and girlish, but as she pretended to listen to her guest she was planning the special celebration she'd make for her screenwriter that night. She'd been waiting to inaugurate the dining alcove of her house at the top of Sunset Plaza Drive for too long, just as she'd put off the decision, in rootless Los Angeles, to buy the house in the first place. Ten thousand dollars down. Her mortgage extended into the future five times as long as her studio contract, but she didn't worry about that.

She made a quick stop at Bagatelle to order food, then made it back to the studio in record time, pulling into her spot at half past two. The place was deserted, except for the secretaries; the men would "wander" back after their three-hour lunches of seafood salad and Perrier. For the briefest instant she pondered the bizarre Los Angeles speech patterns of passive verbs. Everybody was always "wandering" around studios or being instructed to "drop in." You didn't have to be a psych major to understand that passive speech patterns masked not-so-passive behavioral aggression. And at this moment she felt plenty aggressive.

"Any calls?" she asked her secretary, who made a face and handed her an impossibly long list. She wasn't the only executive who'd figured out the phoning-at-lunch trick. Quickly, she perused the callers. A lawyer wanted this week's figures on *Clinton's Boys,* inasmuch as it was time for his client to collect his percentage. A producer calling for a verdict on his latest submission: Another pass, keep trying, she'd say. That was a two-minute call. An inquiry from one of the bankable stars about a book required more care. The studio had once owned it, as it seemed to have once owned everything in print, but she doubted that he knew this; could he really have called because he wanted to work with them?

And three phone calls from her screenwriter, each marked "Urgent." Those she'd return with pleasure.

Going Hollywood

Even though this was business, she dialed his number herself. She would not tell him there had been backstage manipulations; she didn't want him to accuse her of trying to mother his career. If he wanted to believe that he'd probably get his $250,000 because of the work itself, that was a convenient delusion. Without his realizing it, she could continue to be an instrumental force in his career.

"Don't say anything, sit down," he said by way of answering the phone. "The Morris office just called. They've gotten me $375,000 plus a deferment—over at Fox. Isn't that terrific?"

"Terrific!" she exclaimed, with the false cheer perfected at a thousand Hollywood parties and meetings. Then her voice, her spirits sagged. She explained that she was under such pressure at the studio, she didn't feel like making dinner—or seeing him—that night.

She broke the connection and, as she had so many times before, found immediate relief in work, in structure. Because with the head of production primed for a deal, that really was all that mattered. Anxious now, she glanced over the call sheet, looking for a name that might resonate. And then she remembered her first call of the morning, and saw in it her best shot to recover the ground she'd just lost with *Freefall.* So Melvin Dummar was lost to her, was he? Then let Howard Hughes be found.

She buzzed her secretary. "Would you pull together, like right now, the coverage on Beatty's Howard Hughes project? I don't care about the thing itself, just every scrap of gossip about his problems at Warner's. And then leave a message for Warren at the Wilshire. Tell him we'll drop our Melvin Dummar film if he'll promise to come in for a meeting this week. He'll know what *that* means."

She knew what it meant to her: a chance to work with a man who kept his business and personal life separate. She could learn a thing or two from him, she knew, although right now, as she dialed her best friend to ask how she felt about having a little dinner at Mousso & Frank's, she decided that maybe she didn't need to take the work/life dichotomy lessons from Warren Beatty after all. For a moment she tortured herself: Had her screenwriter allowed his agents to use her—once again! —as the hound to trap Fox, and if he had, did she really care about this dumb deal, any deal . . . or this man . . . or anything at all. The enormity of this idea swept over her, just as she hit bottom and realized a certain larger Hollywood truth. So what if the screenwriter had used her as leverage; so too had she been using him. What's more, she didn't detest him. She didn't even dislike him. In fact, she realized, she felt nothing very much at all.

AT THE TOP

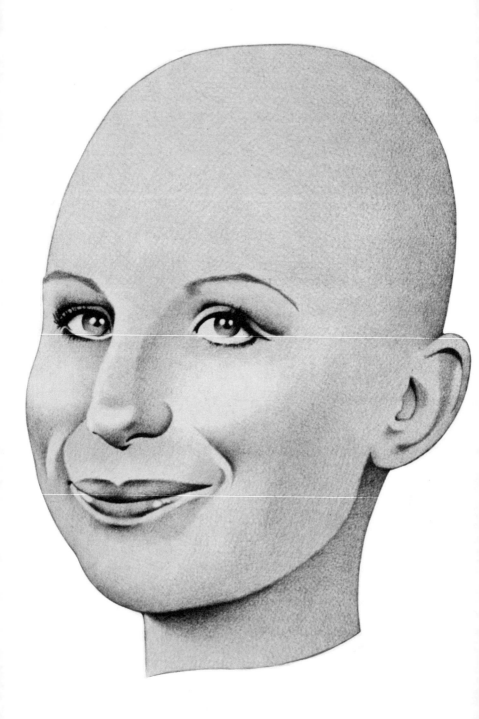

A STAR IS SHORN:
Jon Peters and Barbra Streisand Take On Warner Brothers

I t's early morning in Beverly Hills, and Jon Peters is on the phone with his agent, Hollywood powerhouse Sue Mengers. "Yeah, uh, uh huh . . . that's all you can get?" Peters asks. He stares at himself in the full-length mirror, oblivious to the scene around him: women in smocks having their hair washed, blown out, curled and frosted. "Okay, okay, okay." Peters, a self-styled "street fighter," is, for once, listening. Behind him three assistants are standing over a hair-frost in process, waiting for their teacher's return. A minute ago, Valerie Perrine wandered through the door without an appointment and upset the morning's schedule. But these are minor problems, and this phone call is business.

So Jon Peters is tugging at his black hair, checking himself out in the silvery mirror by the reception desk. Today he's got on the brown-and-gold-checked sweater, platform saddle shoes, and hip-hugging corduroys without underwear. He half turns to see if the extra ten pounds show. And all the while, he's listening to Sue Mengers. Because this morning he has more on his mind than the streaked blonde who worries about getting it on with her gardener (his advice to her: "Go ahead, break out, forget the old-fashioned ways"). For ten years, he's cut hair and put up with the complaints of Bel-Air housewives and Hollywood stars, but now he's taking his own advice and doing a little break-out himself.

Not so little, really. At thirty, the chunky half-Italian, half-Cherokee has risen from having no status as "a kid with dirty underwear going to beauty school" to hair stylist, to husband to actress Leslie Ann Warren, to shopowner, to hair stylist for Barbra Streisand, to boyfriend of Barbra Streisand, to roommate of Barbra Streisand, to record producer for Streisand's new album, *Butterfly,* to Streisand's movie producer. Only the big plum is left— and Sue Mengers is delivering it by phone to the Emperor of Hair on Rodeo Drive. That First Artists–Warner Brothers $5-million musical for 1975, the fourth version of *A Star Is Born,* featuring Barbra Streisand and produced by Jon Peters? Well, it's just found a new director.

"The whole world is waiting to see Barbra's and my story," says new director Jon Peters. And with filming starting in February, the whole world is going to have its chance soon enough.

The only problem was convincing Warner Brothers to let them have their fun.

Fall, 1973

John Dunne and Joan Didion have an idea: Why not write a movie about two rock singers, one on the way up, one on the way down? Make it a love story, make it a tragedy. So, being real writers, they call up their former agent, Dick Shepherd, now head of production at Warner Brothers. "What a good idea," Shepherd says. "I wonder why we didn't think of it."

It just so happens that the Warner Brothers library holds the three previous versions of *A Star Is Born.* Shepherd suggests a remake; it will be easier to convince Warner's to do the project that way. The Dunnes have never seen *A Star Is Born,* not even the Judy Garland version, not even on TV. Anyway, it's the rock world that interests them. They've been traveling around with Jethro Tull and Uriah Heep, cruising the late-night-concert scene, lapping up the details of the Glitter City's underbelly. "Warner's wanted us to see the movie," Dunne said later. "But we assiduously refused to do it. We knew what it was about."

John Foreman is to be the producer. In the 1960s, he produced many of the Paul Newman blockbusters. After *Serpico* became a hit, he decided to make a film about David Durk, Serpico's Ivy League partner. Foreman worked for weeks on the project getting releases from everyone involved. He forgot to get one from David Durk. That movie never got made.

But now Foreman and the Dunnes are working together on their rockumentary, loosely based on *A Star Is Born.* A first-draft screenplay is completed. They submit it to Sue Mengers of Creative Management Associates (CMA), who shuttles it along to another pair of clients: Peter Bogdanovich and Cybill Shepherd. Mengers counted on that director-actress combination to be "a salable package" at the studios; what she didn't count on was the reaction from her writer-clients. The Dunnes would fire her for the transgression, but not before Bogdanovich had had his chance to get his views on the record. "I thought it was awful," Bogdanovich says. "But I showed it to Cybill. She likes to sing. I thought she might like it. She didn't like it much either."

Along comes Mark Rydell, the kinetic director of *The Cowboys* and *Cinderella Liberty.* He loves the material, calls it "a savage look at the rock world." He loves the

Dunnes, calls them "frighteningly brilliant." But Warner's offers him squat for his services. So he agrees to develop the project for free; he's given ninety days to punch up the first draft, cast the film, and get some of those spectacular concert scenes off the drawing board. If he can do all this, he gets to direct the film. For good money. "My agents thought it would work out," he'll explain later.

Somewhere in the deep background, Jon Peters is making space in his closet for Barbra Streisand's clothes. Until he was hired to cut the wig she wore in *For Pete's Sake,* Barbra was sitting home nights, watching TV and playing with her son, Jason. The temperamental Streisand had gone through every hairdresser around when Peters was called in on an emergency basis. "She kept me waiting an hour and a half," Peters will recall. "I said, don't you ever do that again." Barbra liked that: a man who took charge of things. A change from the yes-men and ego-massagers who only fueled every neurosis. So now she's moving in.

March, 1974

Moving into the foreground now, Jon Peters is working with Barbra Streisand on the second pressing of her *Butterfly* album. It is something of a departure from the standard Streisand fare. Jon Peters has decided there is a problem with Barbra's image: dowdiness. She needs to open up and free herself with a shot of rhythm and blues. Barbra has been playing "Ray Stark's mother-in-law" for too long. Time she started to groove—with reggae, David Bowie, and "Let the Good Times Roll." And Jon as the producer. Beautiful. Even Columbia Records thinks so. It's just that they're having some problem getting their vision on tape.

Meanwhile, over at the *Rainbow Road* offices—that's what they're calling *A Star Is Born* now—Rydell and the Dunnes are having trouble finding a cast. Richard Perry, the music producer, is brought in to help out. "Rydell wanted it to be a total collaboration," Perry will recall. "I suggested everybody from Minnelli to Elvis." Casting is not the only problem, though. Perry doesn't like the script: "It really didn't catch the contemporary rock-pop milieu. Everything in it was clichéd. That's when I got misgivings."

An increasingly frantic Rydell pushes for Carly Simon and James Taylor. They demur, saying it's "too close to their relationship." Rydell pushes next for Diana Ross and Alan Price *(O Lucky Man!)*, but Motown's Berry Gordy, who controls Diana Ross, turns him down cold. And Warner's considers Alan Price "too esoteric." Warner's wants its own record stars in the film so the soundtrack album will clean up for the parent corporation.

Rydell is running out of time, and everyone—Warner Brothers, the Dunnes, John Foreman—is after him to "get it on" (Hollywood jargon for making the project happen already). They settle on Kris Kristofferson for the male lead. A female star cannot be found.

This is highly unfortunate. The cameras are supposed to start rolling in September; Warner Brothers is short on product for 1975. *Rainbow Road* could be a '75 Christmas biggie. If only there were a female lead. Forget the fact that there are twenty songs to write, approve, arrange, and stage. And a screenplay still needing a rewrite. And complicated concerts to plan. Warner's wants those cameras rolling. It still hasn't occurred to anyone that the first three versions of *A Star Is Born* never made a dime.

May, 1974

Jon Peters and Barbra Streisand are working on the remodeling of Peters's ranch house in Malibu. *Butterfly* has been salvaged by calling in Kathy Kasper, the music contractor. Peters has agreed to give her co-producer credit for bringing in several new songs and rescoring some of the unusable cuts.

And in the studio, veteran engineer Al Schmitt has been hired by Columbia to remix the album. "Schmitt did three cuts," Barbra says. "I didn't like them." Schmitt goes off the project. But the Columbia executives are happy with the album now; they think "it's not only one of the best, but one of the biggest albums Barbra's ever made." They plan to have Barbra close the August sales convention singing tunes from *Butterfly.*

The album is, finally, manufactured. On the credits, Kathy Kasper's name is nowhere to be found. "It must have been an oversight," Jon Peters will say. Her name will definitely appear on all subsequent pressings.

Summer, 1974

Mark Rydell is on the phone with his agent. The ninety days of his free-development deal are over. Warner Brothers will not "go forward" with him on *Rainbow Road.* Rydell says, "The Dunnes and John Foreman thought I was dragging my heels on the casting. There were a number of people they thought would be good, and if I had said yes, they would have gone ahead with some of their in-house record stars." But he wouldn't, and they didn't, and now Rydell's lawyer is having a tough time collecting the $147 Rydell laid out for research materials and commissary lunches. Warner's isn't making a "courtesy payment" for three months of Rydell's time. In fact, it will take him two months to collect the $147.

But at least the second draft is finished. Warner's finds it vastly improved, a gritty hard-core look at the seamier side of rock. There is, however, no tight relationship between the male and female stars. And while Kristofferson is committed to the project, he has not formally signed.

Warner's now calls director Jerry Schatzberg, whose epigrammatic, often downbeat *Scarecrow* won the Cannes Film Festival for them. A gritty take on the rock world by the Dunnes appeals to him (he'd worked with them before, on *Panic in Needle Park*), and he signs a development deal.

At which point Sue Mengers sends the script to client Barbra Streisand.

"I discovered this project," Jon Peters will say. "I was the one who found it for Barbra and convinced her to do it." He has, he believes, rescued Barbra from her identity crisis; she will be happy to show her fans a "newer, softer Barbra" in a rock-and-roll movie. Already, she is living more like a rock person now that she's left Bel-Air for Jon's funky Malibu ranch. Her hair flows down her back these days. She plants orchids. And plays with the $25,-000 sound system—the hidden jukebox—Peters has thoughtfully stocked with the Streisand sound.

She is also seeing the same Gestalt therapist who treats Jon Peters and Leslie Ann Warren. In fact, they are all

very close. Because Peters is trying "to open myself up."
He is fascinated "by negative feedback," fascinated by
his relationship with Barbra, and fascinated with himself.
"I'm a fella who, when I was nine years old, watched my
father die in front of me," Peters says. "So I know about
death. The character in my movie is a guy who's fighting
all the time and hitting all the time. And he can't relate.
It's the macho story, which is very much me."

The "macho" who runs the two beauty salons—in
Beverly Hills and Encino—started young. His mother is
related to the Paganos, well-known L.A. beauty-salon
owners. When his father died, Jon became "a discipli-
nary problem." He dropped out of school in the eighth
grade, did time in reform school, ran away to Europe,
and got married at fifteen. He left that wife, returned to
Los Angeles, and started hanging around, watching
Gene Shacove—the free-wheeling cut-'em-and-lay-'em
character who supposedly was the inspiration for Warren Beatty's *Shampoo*—work on the heads of the rich and
powerful. Peters learned his lessons well. By twenty-one,
he had met and married Leslie Ann Warren and chopped
her hair off. A year later, *Blow-Up* was released. The mod
style was commercialized. Peters opened his own shop.
A year later, he left Leslie Ann and their son, although
he is still said to have strong feeling for her. And he
installed his mother—who had, only a few years earlier,
shipped him off to reform school—as the receptionist at
the Beverly Hills shop.

So isn't this the perfect time for Sue Mengers to give
Barbra a script about two singers, "trapped by their
money and success, trying to relate to each other and
really get into their feelings," as Peters synopsizes it.
He'd like to change it a little, though.

"Two people fall in love," Peters explains. "She

becomes a super superstar by realizing what the most important thing to both of them is: communicating. Wanting to have children. Not the thousands of agents and press agents and all that stuff that control their life. He's a guy who spent the first thirty years of his life fighting—very aggressive—and then met this woman and fell very much in love and realized that this was his chance. And he really wants to live and he accidentally dies. For us, the understanding of it—through film—is a very heavy thing. Do you know what I mean? That's why the script has to be perfect. Because it has to be right for us."

But Schatzberg, the Dunnes, and John Foreman are not keen on making a $5-million home musical, *Barbra and Jon,* out of their gritty rock story. Not that their opinion means anything—Barbra Streisand, they're made to understand, is interested in starring in *Rainbow Road.* And as her very next project. This is no minor announcement; with the return of the star system, Barbra Streisand is more than just an actress—she is a multinational corporation, the only female star whose whims are as powerful as the edicts of the studio chieftains. In her seven-year film career she has made $12 million—for herself. Her last film, *For Pete's Sake,* was an embarrassment to all concerned, but it brought the money men $11 million. So when Barbra Streisand decides to make a movie, and a musical at that, there are smiles in the corporate offices. Which is why no one at Warner's fights with her about making Jon Peters the producer of *Rainbow Road.*

"Anyone who wonders how a first-time producer can do it," rationalizes Peters, "just has to take a look at the way I produced Barbra's album. Or how I run my beauty salons. I employ three hundred people. I'm a businessman, man, that's all." As a businessman, all he has to do to attach himself to *A Star Is Born* is move into an office and keep his mouth shut, leaving the big decisions to the Dunnes, Foreman, Schatzberg, Kristofferson, and Warner's. He does not do this.

"We loved each other at our first meeting," Schatzberg remembers. "I went out to his ranch; he showed me where he was putting old wood everywhere, the outdoor Jacuzzi . . . we had a good meeting. I didn't see any books, but . . . I went back to New York with the idea that we were going ahead with the project."

Schatzberg and his wife return in July. A big basket of fruit from Barbra and Jon is waiting at the Beverly Hills Hotel. But the Dunnes are worried now: If Barbra agrees to star in the movie, the project will leave Warner Brothers and become a First Artists film.*

Nevertheless, they agree to dovetail the project for Barbra. But although the Dunnes and the Streisand-Peterses all live in Malibu, the Dunnes will not meet with Jon—even for a little story conference—until they have completed the new draft. The Dunnes say they work best alone.

Barbra, meanwhile, is squabbling with Kristofferson about billing. She refuses to see his name above the title

---

*First Artists is a subsidiary of Warner Brothers, a company controlled by the "artists": Dustin Hoffman, Paul Newman, Sidney Poitier, Steve McQueen, and Barbra Streisand. In return for making three pictures without the million dollars front money that any other studio would have to pay them, the stars are given complete creative freedom. They can make whatever movies they want, so long as the budget is under $3 million for a dramatic film, $5 million for a musical. Warners gets the distribution rights, giving First Artists two thirds of the film's negative cost upon delivery of a finished film. And the artists get 25 percent of the gross—a quarter for every dollar the theater-owners return to Warner Brothers—right off the top. They aren't, therefore, encouraged to make small, personal, noncommercial films for their enjoyment and therapy.

with hers. Kristofferson's lawyer, therefore, is holding up the negotiations.

Jon Peters is beginning to feel left out. Schatzberg gets a call from Barbra. She wonders what Schatzberg thinks of Jon playing the male lead. Schatzberg thinks she is kidding.

A hasty meeting is called to discuss this at the ranch. Jon and Barbra keep saying that Jon can play the part better, that the world is waiting to see them together. "I don't want to shoot a documentary about you two," Schatzberg says. John Foreman, now leveraged into the relative Siberia of executive-producership, is silent. Then he reminds Barbra that if the project does go over to First Artists, Kristofferson will still be attached to it. Barbra is angry. "You mean Warner's would really rather have him than me?" she demands. "Can Peters sing?" Schatzberg asks. It is the key question. "No," Jon Peters admits, "but you said you could shoot around me. Like you're going to do with Kristofferson." A weary Schatzberg: "Look, you can do that with a singer to make more energy for his acting. You can't do it with an actor to make it look like he's a singer." The meeting is over. Jon Peters, the haircutter turned record producer turned movie producer, will not make his debut as an actor.

Rainbow Road now seems to be underway. There are fights over production managers, over the music people, but the project is sort of moving ahead. Jon Peters settles into his new office at Barwood, Barbra's company within First Artists, and orders a stereo just like Schatzberg's. The Dunnes are still hung up about the relationship between the male and female leads, but Schatzberg isn't worried. "Screenplays take a lot of work," he says.

Barbra still hasn't signed, though. Nor has Kristofferson. And Warner's has not turned the project over to

First Artists. What does happen is that Dick Shepherd—
the Warner Brothers executive holding the project together—is fired. Then Ted Ashley, Warner Brothers'
president, resigns. The film is now in a curious limbo.
And while Barbra finishes *Funny Lady,* Jon Peters cuts
hair every Wednesday and Saturday in Beverly Hills.

August, 1974

The Dunnes submit their third-draft screenplay. "The
third draft was little more than a rehash of the second
draft," John Dunne recalls. "It's tough to tailor a part for
a star. We were all played out at that point." But as much
as the Dunnes want out, Jon Peters wants them out even
more. Warner Brothers agrees. The Dunnes are given
$125,000 plus 10 percent of the net. "We came out
smelling like a rose," John Dunne says. "I really hope the
movie gets made, we have such a nice chunk of it. And
I'm sure relieved to be out of it."

Jon Peters now has an idea. Or rather, he has a friend
with an idea: Jonathan Axelrod, stepson of screenwriter
George Axelrod, and, just coincidentally, a CMA client.
Sue Mengers has given him the Dunnes' script. Why not
reverse the roles, Axelrod suggests: Let Barbra play the
Norman Maine character, the star on the way down, and
Kristofferson can be Esther Blodgett, the protégée
whose career outstrips her sponsor's. Peters thinks this
is brilliant. He does not know that over the past forty
years three other directors have had the same thought—
William Wellman, George Cukor, and Mike Nichols—
and they have all rejected it.

"My original idea was to reverse the roles, make her
like Janis Joplin," Axelrod says. Schatzberg disagrees.

Peters and Streisand and Schatzberg and Schatzberg's wife have dinner in Laguna Beach. They stop at a restaurant, where Peters remarks, "I've been trying to get into this place for eight years, I'll get in tonight." The maître d' seats them right away. The restaurant is half empty. It is supposed to be a good time, but it doesn't last. Peters insists that the script be turned over to him, that he develop the movie along Axelrod's idea. He tells this to John Calley, new president of Warner Brothers; Warner's still owns those rights to *A Star Is Born.* Calley recalls, "I'd never met Peters before. He came in and said that 'in his and Barbra's view, the screenplay was moving away from being suitable for Barbra.' I agreed with them. Forget about whether the screenplay was good or not, the issue was, is it right for Barbra? He said, in effect, 'It's very simple, either we get to take over the screenplay and make it work for Barbra or we take a walk. It's entirely up to you. Do whatever you like.' We had no real alternatives. We were most anxious to do the film with Barbra." But even if it means losing all artistic control, distributing the movie for First Artists? "I felt," says Calley, "that the worst thing that could happen was that if they took a shot at the screenplay and failed, we'd lose them anyway, but if they succeeded . . ." *If* they succeeded, Warner's would get a Barbra Streisand musical for Christmas, following her projected triumph in *Funny Lady,* in a year when Warner's isn't long on product.

"I told Jerry [Schatzberg] to stay loose and see what the two of them were able to do with the screenplay," Calley says. "He thought about it overnight and called me the next day and said, 'Listen, I don't want anyone else developing my screenplays.' " Jerry Schatzberg is walking off the movie. He is the fifth casualty.

Fall, 1974

Jonathan Axelrod is working on the fourth draft. He has turned in fifty-five pages of the new screenplay. He has not reversed the roles. But Barbra loves it. More: Jon loves it. Barbra has agreed to sign on the basis of the first third of this script. Peters starts interviewing new directors: Arthur Hiller, Hal Ashby. Warner Brothers has not completely turned the project over to First Artists, although First Artists funds are paying Axelrod for writing the script that Barbra will agree to star in. To be very literal, Barbra has commissioned a screenplay for her company when the underlying rights to it are still owned by another company.

"The conflict came," Peters says, "when I decided *I* wanted to direct it. It's a story I felt only I could tell. I wanted to deal with it and not interpret it through another person. Barbra felt this was a wise choice, too." Did Warner Brothers agree? "I don't want to get into any negatives," Peters insists. "There were negotiations that went on for three months. "It bounced back and forth because they wanted to control it, but then Barbra and First Artists had their way because Freddie Fields [President of CMA] wanted it at First Artists as well."

The bottom line, of course, is Barbra. Barbra wants the movie at First Artists with her boyfriend producing, directing, and co-writing it—Barbra gets it. Freddie Fields and Sue Mengers are her agents, and they are very powerful and persuasive, but now that Jon is throwing his weight around, who knows? He is capable of getting angry with Barbra's agents, and then he will say to her, "Get rid of these assholes. You have me. What do you need anybody else for?" Already Joyce Haber has been running items in her column in the Los Angeles *Times* about Mengers's worries with this Jon Peters situation. Naturally Sue Mengers puts pressure on John Calley; she wants to keep Barbra happy.

Calley makes the decision to turn it all over to Barbra.

Winter, 1974

Barbara finally finishes *Funny Lady.* She and Jon can now work full-time on *Rainbow Road.* Their first move: firing Jonathan Axelrod. He has, apparently, failed. Peters feels he needs "meatier dialogue." He says, "Axelrod was the right person at the beginning, because he was my interpreter. What you read in that script, I wrote. Now I need a real writer." Why don't he and Barbra take a crack at a rewrite? "We're talkers," says Peters, "not writers."

Sue Mengers, therefore, is not concentrating on her bratwurst and beans as she lunches at the Polo Lounge. At the next banquette, Everett Ziegler, the literary agent, is having lunch with Bob Solo, the new Warner Brothers head of production. "Hey, Ziggy, you literary lion," Mengers yells over, "we need a writer for *A Star Is Born.*" "How about asking John Dunne to suggest one?" Ziggy replies. "Come on, I'm serious—there's *money* involved," Mengers insists. But Ziegler is not enthusiastic about finding a writer for that project. He seems to think the whole thing is a joke.

So Jon Peters starts interviewing screenwriters. He speaks with a soft-spoken television writer. But the writer cuts the meeting short and leaves, mumbling that Peters is an idiot, that he wouldn't be caught dead writing for him, even if it means passing up a Barbra Streisand credit.

There is also a problem with the music. Richard Perry —the first choice of Rydell, Schatzberg, and Barbra—has been meeting with each new director of *Rainbow Road* since winter of 1973. "In my last phone conversation with Jon Peters," Perry recalls, "he said, wouldn't it be great if the two of us could co-direct, be a real team, y'know?" Perry never gets another phone call.

Jack Nietsche, who scored *Performance,* is now called in. He had worked for a few days on the *Butterfly* album but flipped out; Peters thinks he'll do fine on *Rainbow Road.* He is, however, replaced a few weeks later by Rupert Holmes, an accomplished New York composer-arranger who once had a number-one hit with a song about cannibalism in mine shafts. Peters plunges into the work with him in December.

Now all Jon Peters needs is a director of photography and a good editor. And to lose the ten pounds he's gained over the last six months. He sits in the Warner Brothers commissary, brooding about his movie. He does not order even half a grapefruit. "This is a young movie, young idea, young talents," he blurts out. "People in this town have it in for me because I'm young, y'know what I mean? And I'm a bit uptight about directing this film, this is a big project, y'know?" Yes, but with that good editor, good script, and good cameraman, someone suggests, he'll be the equal of half the working directors in Hollywood. "Exactly, that's just what I think," Peters agrees. "That's why my editor is Dede Allen."

This creates a major silence at the table. Because Dede Allen, who edited *Serpico* and *Bonnie and Clyde,* is about as good as you can get. Maybe Peters knows what he is doing after all. But when Peters returns to his office and the phone rings—a call from Dede Allen—Jon Peters's press agent takes the visitors outside. "Jon wants to take the call in private," he explains. "He's never spoken with Dede Allen before."

Dede Allen turns Peters down. She suggests her young former assistant. He is twenty-four. He has never before edited a feature film. Jon Peters says, "Great! This is a young movie, we need young ideas, we need young talent."

But by now, naturally, Peters is getting what he'd call "hassled." His sentences are delivered rapid-fire, with the grammar increasingly slurred. He no longer prefaces his sentences with "Barbara and I feel . . ." Now he begins with "I said . . ." or "I told Barbra . . ." He is pulling no-shows with writers, music people, and his production crew.

In fact, Jon Peters is now yelling. "Directing is a thing I've done my whole life! It's getting people to do what I want them to do!" He kicks rocks as he strides around the fourteen-acre Malibu ranch. "If you had seen this place when I started, the fact that it was all dirt."

And in truth, the house is a cathedral-ceilinged, *House Beautiful* vision of ranch living: a powder room with marble counters, a fur lounging bed covered with antique pillows that doubles as the living-room couch, and a bathtub built from stones cemented together. Barbra's things are everywhere. Boas. Hats. Pictures. Clothes. Health foods. Outside there are signs of expansion: Land has been roped off for gardens, and there is a hole where a natural rock swimming pool—a large outdoor version of the bathtub—waits to be finished. Through all this, the street fighter who used to work out at the Main Avenue gym in downtown Los Angeles struts around like Nixon eyeing improvements at San Clemente. It does not matter to him that Joyce Haber snipes in his direction every time he says or does anything. He does not care that the men who lunch at La Scala and the Bistro, the men who run the studios, say things like "Thank God those two aren't on our backs." He is not sensitive to the letters from angry First Artists stockholders who demand to know what is going on. He is not deterred by the news that his name brings snorts of laughter just about anywhere it's brought up in Bel-Air. What Jon Peters appreciates very well is that he is living with a large entertainment corporation; as he says, "I've got the power, man, I've got them by the balls."

That kind of power is rarely benign. It is not enough for Jon Peters to mastermind the career of his private conglomerate. He is not satisfied with a minor role as Barbra's shield, giving her the privacy she says she now wants. Yes, he sees himself as the take-charge guy in her business life—he says, "I have in my pluses [sic] a woman who, if she would get up on the screen and smile, the movie would do twenty million dollars"—but even more, he sees himself as the lead in their larger-than-life movie, the one that so closely resembles *A Star Is Born.*

Jon Peters, therefore, believes he is on the way up, all the way up. The only question now is the quality of the ascent. Which is why *A Star Is Born* must be made his way —because only he knows the special message he has for his best supporting actress. "What I'm really saying in this film is to Barbra," Peters explains. "Which is: You better check your act and see if it's the money or the success which is the most important thing. Are your goals the things that you really want to achieve? You gotta evaluate all the time. Because the danger in dreams is that you just might get them."

"What can I say? He makes Barbra happy. She's never looked better in her life," comments Barbra's agent, Sue

Mengers. Barbra is a survivor; she could care less that the SEC's comment on the First Artists setup was "Giving performing artists creative control over their films represents a significant departure from traditional industry practice." After all, you don't get further away from "traditional industry practice" than Jon Peters.

But once you commit yourself to someone like Peters, your most immediate problem is pleasing him. Because Jon Peters can be a very moody person. "Emotional," he'd say. Like at the Christmas party of Jon Peters, Inc., when he stands before a roomful of his employees and chokes up. "This is a very sad day for me," Peters says. "I won't be coming into the shop any more to cut hair. I have to spend all my time for the next year with this film, y'know?" It's very heavy for him. And, by extension, for her. "Barbra wishes that she could be here too, but she was afraid she would cry."

But there is a bright side. Jon Peters has found new writers. He hopes they'll be The Last Writers. "We had the most beautiful weekend with them," he burbles. "We're going up to Big Sur with them. We're going to throw away everything we've done up to now and start over again. We're going to make this a love story. They're the most beautiful people, and the love they have for each other is the same feeling as Barbra and I have for each other. These last five months with Jonathan [Axelrod] have taught me what I don't want to do with this film. Now we're going to make it much closer to the 1936 version, the one with Janet Gaynor. That was magic." For a moment, Jon Peters hesitates as if—for the first time—he's thinking about the enormity of this task. Then, finally he speaks. "Yes . . . *magic.* That's what we want to achieve."

Marie Brenner

A STAR LIVES ON

During the tortuous years of making *A Star Is Born,* there were countless stories written about the difficulties of working with Barbra Streisand and her lover/producer/former hairdresser Jon Peters; they were tyrants no one could please. Writer after writer, beginning with Joan Didion and John Dunne, bit the dust. A second director was called in, and he lost final editing rights over his film. At one point Streisand told Warner Brothers she wanted Peters, whose apprenticeship in films had been nonexistent, to co-star as well as produce. I'm familiar with all of this because I covered the story for *New Times.* The cover of the issue it appeared in showed a drawing of a bald Barbra Streisand accompanied by the line: A STAR IS SHORN.

Jon Peters sent me a grotesque floral arrangement.

With this history, I couldn't wait to get my hands on what I was sure would be the casualty of all the attendant warfare: the film itself. But I have a problem: I liked *A Star Is Born.*

It is not the gritty inside look at the rock world that Didion and Dunne proposed. It is not, as Peters promised, a Streisand-Peters home movie flung on the big screen. It is not even, really, *A Star Is Born* (this is the third remake of the story). What it is, is the quintessential Barbra Streisand movie, about the brassy waif with a heart of gold and a voice to match and how she fights her way for love and a rightful prominence in the world. It's every Barbra Streisand movie you've ever seen, only more so. Mostly it's *The Way We Were,* but with music.

Kris Kristofferson is the foundation of the picture, though, not Streisand. The film opens with one of his concerts. He's late. The crowd is stomping for him. A

Frisbee arcs down from the balcony. Kristofferson's limo pulls into the backstage area. He's tired, run-down, but —there's no other way to say it—incredibly humpy. He strides down the corridor, oblivious to the excitement; he's a man on his way to work. Two hits of cocaine, a tilt of the bourbon bottle, one stride, and he's on-stage, seen from behind as the lights and the applause turn him on. And then he sings a perfectly inane song ("Are you a figment of my imagination or am I a figment of yours?" it begins), and you wonder why all these kids think he's so hot when it's obvious he's a marginal talent bent on destroying himself.

That's not the only thing that doesn't make sense. After his concert, a wired Kristofferson goes to a little night spot where Barbra's performing with two black backup singers. (Barbra's the one with the frizzy hair— a joke the filmmakers apparently couldn't resist.) Her voice belongs in a cathedral, not in a dive. Kristofferson falls for her, self-destructs for her love, and puts his own career on the line to give her the kind of break that every chorus girl dreams about.

The dialogue is often painful. "Where to?" the chauffeur asks Kristofferson. "Back about ten years," he answers. The dubbing of Streisand's songs is too often out of sync. Streisand's acting works against her lines; when she tells Kristofferson, "I can take all the tenderness you've got, as a matter of fact," she's tougher than a bouncer at a rock concert. Every time she turns around, she's got on a new costume.

None of this matters. Once *A Star Is Born* gets into the love story, that fascination Streisand exerts over her audiences manages to overpower critical distance. When Barbra tells her manager, the man Kris made rich, that he should help Kris in his need, she suddenly stops and says, "This sucks! Why do I have to pitch you?" you feel her anger. Always, she repels but mesmerizes—could she be transferring about Elliott Gould? When she weeps over Kris Kristofferson's dead body, we weep too —but are we weeping for the brilliant singing career she's trashed in service to her ego?

Frank Pierson, who deserves combat pay for taking on the direction of this picture (after Jon Peters decided it was too much for him to handle), has joined with cinematographer Robert Surtees to create a film as seductive to look at as its actors are compelling to watch. With an enormous assist from Kristofferson, who tries to show on-screen a love for Barbra he is said to have felt only rarely during the shooting, they have created a vehicle for Hollywood's most difficult star that—through endless close-ups—enables her to parade her narcissism *and* even win our sympathies. John Updike once said that anybody can make a case for himself, if you listen long enough. He might have just seen *A Star Is Born.*

SUE MENGERS:
The Hottest Agent in Hollywood

Y ou could hear the screaming and the banging and the swearing all the way out on the winding driveway high up on Bel-Air Road where yesterday's rain puddles were steaming out in the California sunshine. Sue Mengers, the Hollywood agent, was in her stocking feet and together with one of her two Portuguese maids ("the dummies," she calls them) was shoving her weight—no negligible force—against her warped outer front door, trying to get it unstuck. "Honeee . . . Just a minute, honeee . . . Come *on*, push, Yolanda . . ." Sue Mengers or Yolanda (or maybe both of them) was panting in the courtyard. The front door— the one that used to seal off Zsa Zsa and now insures the privacy of the hottest agent in Hollywood—wouldn't budge. So, Sue Mengers was getting angry and was pushing even harder. Outside the sun was glistening off her Mercedes, the one she'd be wheeling out in later that morning, to have—along with star client Barbra Streisand—the first look anyone's had at *Funny Lady*, the sequel to *Funny Girl.* That is, if she could get her front door open. *"God damn this ——— place,"* Sue Mengers yelled through the white brick and the dark wood; then, in a burst, she tumbled out, her acres of blond hair clamped Saturday-morning style to the top of her head with a

Lady Ellen clip, and she was looking a little sticky, like a marshmallow with glasses—or, as someone once said, like a Rona Barrett Blow-Up Doll—but then, she was out of sorts because the front door of her new $300,000 home—the one with the seven bathrooms—had been giving her trouble.

But not like the trouble Lew Wasserman and "that black tower at Universal," as Sue calls them, had been giving her. Just that week Wasserman, Universal's president, had backed out on *Bugsy Siegel,* client Peter Bogdanovich's—he thought—upcoming epic about the thirties gangster. Bogdanovich, who had already put in months with producers Dick Zanuck and David Brown, learned that he was off the picture—his budget had come in too high—so now they weren't about to rush payment on his $600,000 pay-or-play deal. (In the movie business the term "pay or play" means one receives the full contracted fee for a film whether the project gets made or not.) Peter Bogdanovich, no Hollywood shlocker, and by extension Sue Mengers, no third-rate flesh peddler, had been zapped. For any agent, this is a problem. For Suzy (as her mother calls her) Mengers, age thirty-nine, the world's most powerful female agent, this was more than a problem. Tsuris, she'd call it. And the way Suzy would deal with Bogdanovich's tsuris was the way she's solved everything blocking her way, including the front door. "I just always pushed harder than anyone else," she explains.

So now she's padding through her big white house, the one with the marble floors and all the windows looking down at Los Angeles tanning below. And Sue's listening for the phones to ring, always listening for the phones. First, it could be her screenwriter-husband, Jean-Claude Tramont (formerly: Schwartz), jangling her from Paris, where he was waiting for her to join him for their second honeymoon. Their first trip was four years ago, but it didn't count, mainly because John Calley, Warner Brothers' president, also then a newlywed, had been tagging along. And even on that trip Sue had been obsessed by the phones. "When we got to Mykonos," Sue remembers, "John and I raced each other for the telephone, and I think I spent most of my wedding trip locked in a phone booth."

So when those subtle chimes start tinkling this morning on Bel-Air Road, if it's not Jean-Claude, then it would probably be one of five main characters in the Bogdanovich drama: Irwin Winkler, the producer; Jack Schwartzman, the lawyer; Peter Bogdanovich, the client; Freddie Fields, the boss (CMA's president); or David Begelman, the studio head (Columbia). Because Sue has "been living with these guys for the past five days" trying to put a lock on a deal—a brand-new deal—that will make up for the royal zetz Universal had given her and her client by canceling *Bugsy Siegel.*

She won't be disappointed. Sue, Suzy, or Susan Mengers, endless Earth Mother and homicidal deal-maker, always comes through for her children. Which isn't so hard when you have eighteen overachievers like Barbra Streisand, Peter Bogdanovich, Cybill Shepherd, Gene Hackman, Tuesday Weld, Gore Vidal, Herb Ross, Bob Fosse, Ryan O'Neal, Faye Dunaway, Ali MacGraw, Candy Bergen, Tatum O'Neal, Tony Perkins, Sidney Lumet, Arthur Penn, Stanley Donen, and Cher. These are clients any agent would kill for. Their billings alone mean about $1.5 million a year to Sue's employers, International Creative Management, the talent conglomerate that's just taken over CMA (Creative Management Associates), where Sue had been considered queen. She hopes the merger won't change things much. Sue's star-studded client list has brought her a new three-year contract, which, figuring in stock options, expense accounts, and salary, has raised her income to around $175,000 a year. That's more than most studio heads earn, more than enough to allow her to give party after party—something she's famous for—all in the Bel-Air house she's fought so hard to get.

Still, she's not taking any chances. So on this Bog-danovich deal, the one that's breaking open just as *Bugsy Siegel* is falling apart, Sue is poised by the phones, eating poached eggs in her glassed-in breakfast room. There's a lot at stake with this project: a script called *Starlight Parade* (it would be released as *Nickelodeon*) written by W. D. Richter *(Slither)* about the early days of Hollywood—*a silent film,* yet—and it's needing a rewrite, plus it's un-budgeted (which in Hollywood means the final costs could go through the roof), but Bogdanovich *likes* it and likes the writer, *wants to do it as his next film;* so Sue is poised for action. She knows she's got a "hot one." This will be Bogdanovich directing a paean to Hollywood, his favorite subject, so she's sure there's no way he'll make this one another *Daisy Miller.* Sue knows it and the studio heads know it, so she's going to nail them to the wall. The terms are astronomical: a record $750,000 for her boy-wonder director. And on an enforceable pay-or-play basis too. Chutzpah, she'd call it, but why not, it's what the traffic can bear. Now she's at her absolute peak—that feeling of *I know we're going to get it, honey* is beginning to come up from her spine, so she's calm for a minute and looks out toward her pool, down the knoll, a football field away. And she sighs. "I wish it weren't all the way down there. Every time you want to go swimming, it's like shlepping to Jones Beach." But mostly she's watch-

ing the phone or buzzing Yolanda to bring in the Sweet
'n Low, waiting for any one of her four lines to start
lighting up. One direct to ICM, one her private hot line,
and the others merely unlisted.

She doesn't have long to wait. "Honey," she tells Irwin
Winkler, the first caller, "Frank Wells [Warner's chair-
man] turned us down. Honey, *don't worry.* I'm having
dinner with David Begelman and Peter Guber [Co-
lumbia's chairman and vice-president of production] tonight." Her voice drops to baby talk, her Fu Manchu
fingernails tap on the table. "See, honee, I'm working all
the time for you . . ." And she is, because that same
evening she's locked the deal at Columbia and gotten
everything Bogdanovich wants. All that remains are the
fine points. And still the client will get hourly status
reports. To Bogdanovich, three days later: "I'm available
for this any time of the day or the night . . . The major
things have been resolved, sweetie, so the worst thing
that can happen is that we'll have the conference call in
the morning."

Business done, she can turn on the mother again.
"Honey, honey, tell me again that you're happy." Sue is
lounging on her king-size bed with the hand-crocheted
oatmeal bedspread, which she lives in constant terror of
scarring with a ubiquitous Gitane. She's teasing Bogdanovich. "Do you think it's easy to get you a job?
Honey, *I'm kidding* . . . Well, when you sit right down to
it and you say the words 'pay or play'—*without a screenplay*
—well, they all want it in theory, but when they want it
when you talk about the facts . . . Well, that's pretty damn
good." Sue is looking out at L.A.'s lights through her
bedroom's terrace door, the phone cradled to her ear.
"WHAT FACTS? *The pay-or-play, honey, and for a very large
sum of money, too, you know?*" and for a split second the

world's most powerful lady agent is frowning, but still she isn't changing her tone, she isn't letting on to her prodigy director that maybe he's kvetching at Aunt Suzy a little too much.

The phone calls, the deal-making, the parties, the house in Bel-Air. "It all sounds terribly glammmorous," Sue would say, letting her tongue roll on the *mmm* an extra beat. And it does all sound awfully *glammmorous*— even to Sue. This is the kind of copy the fan magazines crave. The Mengers Mystique, self-created, the wit, the charm, the warmth, the aggression, the machetelike honesty, the scheming, the vulnerability, the neurosis. If only the blonde lady agent at the center of the firestorm —the one who's fueling the fantasies of the next decade's Sammy Glicks—would realize that she can let up just a little. Nobody is going to force her to take the subway back where she came from (the Bronx) or even further back—to the boat she and her parents squeaked out of Germany on in 1939. The Mengerses—Sue's an only child—settled in Utica, New York, where they took menial jobs, since they couldn't speak English. Four years later Sue's father committed suicide. Then she and her mother moved to the Bronx, where Sue went to school and her mother supported them by working as a bookkeeper. It's a soap opera of a background, so twenty-five years later, when the Portuguese maids serve the little-girl-refugee breakfast in bed—with a daily fresh rosebud —Sue sees the ritual as more than just a nouveau-riche indulgence. "It all has to do with having a working mother and being left very much alone," Sue explains. "When I was a little girl and I'd wake up, I'd be all alone in the house. On the kitchen table would be a glass of milk and a muffin. For me, breakfast in bed was the symbol. The thing that was really important."

But before the breakfast-in-bed came the Getting There. The Saturday afternoons Sue spent in the movies, like those other kids from the boroughs, Rona Barrett and David Geffen. Those days shaped plenty of dreams. If the Bronx teenagers couldn't go to Dalton, didn't know about Viola Wolf's Dance Classes, well, maybe they could pick up what Sue would later call "class" by watching Greer Garson—all lacquered nails and blonde gentility—gliding across a pastel drawing room flickering there in the dark. Watching the Lombards, the Hepburns, the Bacalls, inhaling their smoky Hollywoodized appeal; those kids in the Roxy knew there had to be something more *glammmorous* than their own Grand Concourse. After all, who knew better than the dream-shapers themselves, those moguls who were also Grand Concourse graduates. Sue explains: "When you grow up and you wake up and you're out of high school and the only people you know are your family, who have no connections, or your friends, who are getting married to young dentists or are working as typists in the General Cigar Company, and all you know are other secretaries who are saving up their money like you to go off on weekends to meet guys at the Concord, you wonder: How am I ever going to climb out of all this? I guess what I'm really trying to say is: *I had no help.*"

But you don't need help when you have raw nerve and brains, plus the Mengers style. So when she spotted the ad for "receptionist, theatrical agency," she grabbed the job. "I never grew up wanting to be an agent," Sue will explain. "I grew up wanting to marry a nice Jewish boy and have children." Only nice Jewish boys don't marry Hepburns or Bacalls, and if they do, not ones like Sue, because, as she says, "I was no beauty."

From her desk at MCA, she saw plenty. "I saw the

agents going to opening nights. I began slowly—like someone with their nose pressed against the bakery window with no money to buy a cake—and I began to see life around me as a secretary. I saw those agents going out to lunch and dinner with all the people that I wanted to know." From MCA, Sue went to work at Baum & Neuborn, a free-lance theatrical agency of the fifties which had built its reputation on hustle, and from there to the William Morris office with a ten-dollar raise, where the style wasn't pastrami at the desk and yelling "I can book 'em for two weeks at the Music Center," as it had been at Baum & Neuborn. "That's where I learned how to be chic," Sue says of her William Morris apprenticeship.

Still she was waiting for Prince Charming. "I saw those lovely ladies at the Morris office in their mink coats having their lovely lunches at the Colony. They were doing all the things I thought you had to be married to do. Trips to Europe. Theater. Dinners with glammmorous people. I began to think—you know, there was no Women's Lib then—that gee, there are things going on out there that you don't have to be married to do. And that's when I started getting ambitious."

Which didn't solve her problems. "One weekend my mother and I went away to Atlantic City, and I remember we were walking on the boardwalk, talking about nothing in particular, and suddenly I started to cry. It was all those frustrations of wanting to be included in a world that I didn't know how to get included in. My mother said, 'There's something wrong with you, why don't you go to one of those head doctors? We have a cousin who's a psychologist—she's a relative, so she won't think you're crazy . . .' and I went to that woman and I got this feeling of great relief, as if I could talk to someone objective. It helped me. Analysis helped me hold on till I could make it."

It was a rocky road. "I remember when I was a secretary being asked to deliver a script to Tyrone Power's apartment. Tyrone Power! The whole way up on the Madison Avenue bus—I remember I got out at Madison Avenue and Seventy-second—I had this fantasy that Tyrone Power would come to the door and say, 'Why don't you come in and stay for supper?' and then he'd fall madly in love with me. Of course, the minute I got there the doorman said, 'I'll take care of that, thanks.' I remember that feeling of total, total frustration, that I couldn't even get in to hand him the script. That terrible feeling of being left out all the time."

Sue determined to overcome. She made herself into a caricature—anything to stay at the center of the action—then found herself ripe for even greater parody (the predatory agent Dyan Cannon played in *The Last of Sheila* was pure Mengers). "I was walking through the Morris office one day," recalls an agent who worked with her in the fifties. "Sitting in the reception area were the Marquis Chimps, the ones who used to be at Radio City. They were Morris clients and were quietly sitting with their trainer, waiting to see their agent. Suddenly Sue appeared, spotted the apes, lifted her skirt, and said, 'Monkey, want to ———?"

After years of working as "Tillie the Toiler," as Sue calls it, she stopped typing and went into partnership with Tom Korman, one of her co-workers from the Baum & Neuborn days. That was 1963. Sue's first year as a full-fledged agent, she was bringing in $150 a week, but "I had my own secretary; someone to say 'Miss Menger's office.' That and the breakfast in bed were my symbols that at last I was getting there." After the secretary came the mink coat she bought on time payments (always the obsession with outside appearances), then came the hanging out at Sardi's, shoving her calling card into actors' faces while her eyelashes would blink and the baby voice would come out, "Hi, I'm Sue Mengers, I'd like to represent you." Obsessive-compulsive, but it all paid off when Freddie Fields, then president of CMA, hired her away from Korman, bringing her into his New York office.

Which lasted about one month. This period in Sue's life, around 1966, was probably her most manic. Flushed with success from her partnership with Korman, the little girl from the Bronx was at last in a "class place," and as a full agent. Naturally, she went a little crazy. Many stories spring from this period—the time she tried to convince the *Cabaret* producers to hire her personal client Anthony Newley when they had already settled another CMA star, Joel Grey; then, lesson not learned, she pushed her own client Kim Darby over Liza Minnelli, also of CMA, for *Sterile Cuckoo*.

There's honor even among agents, and the New York CMA crew hated her guts. And told their boss, Freddie Fields, "If she's so great, why don't you let her prove it out in California?" Off she went.

On the West Coast, the Mengers style—the brashness, the *mazel*—stayed practically the same, but out there it worked.

But not without a struggle. Here's Sue in her first year on the Coast, pulling up alongside a stoplight next to Burt Lancaster. "Oh, Mr. Lancaster," Sue yahoos out her window, "who represents you?" "IFA," he replies. "Not for long," Sue yells as she vrooms off down Sunset. Lancaster resisted the pitch; there were many who didn't. And of her early signers, only a few—Rod Steiger,

Going Hollywood

Dick and Paula Benjamin, Dyan Cannon, Christopher Plummer—have jumped ship. Bogdanovich signed up early after *Targets* because Sue clipped an article about the promising young director. She worked on Tony Perkins for six months ("I think he thought I was some funny pisher from the Bronx," Sue will explain), until she convinced him one day over lunch at the Plaza. Ryan O'Neal signed because she strolled up to him once at a party and blurted, "When are you going to get rid of your dumb asshole of an agent?"

Aggression like this goes especially well rewarded by Freddie Fields, who has a computer programmed to break an agency dollar into percentages that tell him how much each of his agents is worth. "For signing a client, 50 percent," Field explains. "For holding a client, 25 percent. And for selling a client, another 25 percent." Sue is a signer, and in the deal-making process an opener; she brings the elements together, but doesn't take it all the way to the fine points before the closing. Meaning she scores about 95 percent.

For a star, she is simply as good as it gets. "I'd just come out from the Coast," says one of her clients, "I was really starting to hit. A few TV things, a small movie or two, then the one big part and my name below the title. I had this awful feeling that at any moment someone was going to take it all away—rip my stills from the walls. I thought they'd pull my film from the theaters and slam in *The Poseidon Adventure.* Then I got a call, 'Hi, I'm Sue Mengers, I'd like to represent you.' I think that's when I knew everything was going to be okay."

And it was. Because in a town filled with players, having La Mengers as your agent is the ultimate in gamesmanship. Because her hustling never stops. Her clients, from the beginning, got incredible deals. For Bogdanovich, even before *The Last Picture Show* was released, she put together *What's Up, Doc?*, persuading Barbra to take the lead without seeing a script. (She later had to smooth Barbra's ruffled feelings when Bogdanovich put her through the indignity of line readings.) And she made sure Bogdanovich saw *Love Story* in a theater with a real audience so he'd see Ryan O'Neal was more than some *Peyton Place* dummy.

Then there was *Paper Moon,* when Bob Evans and O'-Neal weren't speaking and, worse, Bogdanovich thought the material too trivial to consider—unless Tatum and Ryan O'Neal were promised as the leads. Sue badgered Bogdanovich: "Make this deal, I want to close it tonight." Evans was, after all, leaving for New York the next day. Before he took off, the deal was signed.

Bob Evans will laugh about the times Sue tried to ram Ryan O'Neal down his throat for *The Godfather* and pitched Barbra to him as the perfect Daisy for *Gatsby,* but his favorite Homicidal Sue story is from the casting of *Chinatown.* It was Faye Dunaway versus Jane Fonda right down to the wire for him, with Fonda a slight favorite and Sue pushing her client, Dunaway. And pushing her hard. "If you don't give me an offer in twenty-four hours," Sue screamed at Evans, "Faye is signing with Arthur Penn to do *Night Moves.*" Evans bit, signed Dunaway, and learned two days later that Penn hadn't even been considering his new star. "As close friends as we are," Evans marveled, "she tried so hard for her clients that she actually lied to me. Her best friend, she still lied to me!"

Another triumph was negotiating the astronomical $1.25 million Gene Hackman received for replacing George Segal in Stanley Donen's *Lucky Lady.*

As Sue's successes and reputation grow, so do her anxieties. There are her worries about media burn—

she's been called a ball-cutter, a Sherman tank, a monster lady. Sue says she's tired of being used as "local color" and couldn't have been more astounded when *Vogue* recently named her a Vital Woman. "Can you believe me with Nancy Kissinger, Betty Ford, and that writer, what's her name, Erica *Yawng?* It's like a dream come true." The trick, of course, is to manipulate the press. When Mike Wallace on *60 Minutes* asked her a question about Dyan Cannon, she didn't want to answer. She looked at him while the cameras rolled and called her ex-client an obscene name, calculated to wind up on the cutting-room floor.

These days, the question Sue is asking herself is, now that she's climbed to the top, can she stay there?

She hopes so. So there are the parties, her chance to show that she knows the right people. And if in the process a deal or two can be talked about, well, that's just one more way to justify her $40,000-a-year expense account to—as she calls him—"Uncle Freddie." "She gets the best cast and serves the worst food in the world," says Bob Evans. "She gets caterers that I think come from the Salvation Army." Frank Yablans, former Paramount president, was even blunter. He called her food "camel shit," but he always came back.

The parties are only half of it. There's an axiom in Hollywood now that the hotter you are, the less you need an agent. It's deal by complicated deal; the starlets aren't waiting around for their agents to tell them how many years Mr. Mayer wants them for and for what money. Now, besides the agent, lawyers and business managers are involved, and everybody's taking a chunk out of the actor's astronomical dollars. It's really all about levels: The hotter you are, the more scripts will get funneled your way. The more sophisticated you are about the business, the less you rely on Sue Mengers, *on any agent,* for advice. "Do you think I depend on my agent for anything?" Peter Bogdanovich says. Then why do the clients stay? The bottom line is: Why not? "I've had that conversation with my lawyers about whether you just need a reader and legal advice, but really, for the difference in money—it's all deductible—it hardly pays not to have an agent." This from fiercely loyal Gene Hackman. It's not without reason that Sue gets clutched in the stomach every time her phone rings late at night.

Perhaps she understands that she gives people plenty to talk about. Her jealousy, for one thing. Joyce Haber tells the story about the time she planned to write up a new lady agent and Sue phoned her, screaming, "How dare you undercut me this way?" (That story never ran.) For another, her constant need for attention. A *Time* correspondent came to write about the New Hollywood and ICM's stars and, after a lunch at which Mengers spoke only of her own terrific history, went back to New York to immortalize the agent in *Time.* Others fault her for her savage (they say "heartless") honesty, like the time she told a client, now at William Morris, "Listen, I couldn't get you a film like *The Godfather* to star in. Your last two films have been bombs. You're fifth on everybody's list." Others cite her yenta style of nagging. "It worries me sometimes the way she drops little bombs," says client Gene Hackman. "Like 'We've got three pictures for the spring and we don't know if any of them are going to be successful. It sure would be nice if we could get a new one locked up right away.'"

Even Sue-the-Good quips are swapped like baseball cards. Her wit, usually self-deprecating: "What does Ryan O'Neal want to spend time with me for, I'm like his Aunt Yetta." To Henry Kissinger: "My mother thinks it's wonderful the way you treat your parents, but you should take them out of Washington Heights." The endless Earth-Mothering: (on the phone with Bogdanovich) "Honey, what are you getting X-rayed for? An *ulcer?* Honey, will you please stop working so hard? *Please,* honey?" The vulnerability: At one of her bi-weekly dinner parties, at the table-for-twelve, Sue will whine, "This is a terrible party, everybody's having a terrible time, there are no stars here." And, of course, flanking the table will be John Calley, Candy Bergen, Jack Nicholson, Gore Vidal, Rex Reed.

Classically, you'd look at a life like Sue Mengers's and conclude that if only there had been a man in her life, some of her edges would smooth. And Sue—who once described herself as "Queen of the Fag Hags"—would almost agree. "I was sure I'd never get married. I never thought anyone would cope with my drive. There's something very asexual about being an agent. Oh, one or two men along the way thought it might be perverse and interesting to try to challenge me—after all, it wasn't like I was Johnny Belinda—but it was always on that level because it's sure not any turn-on to talk business with a woman."

Then, in 1972, she went to a party at Anne Ford's—whose sister, Charlotte, had always been Sue's unattainable physical and social ideal—and there was Jean-Claude. When he kissed her hand, she thought he was a gigolo, because, "after all, what would anyone so handsome be looking at me for, I was no glamor queen." He wasn't a gigolo, but a writer. His first produced screenplay, *Ash Wednesday,* was released right before their wedding.

So although Sue's trademark has always been her vehement "I hate what I do," there is, for the first time, maybe some real meaning now when she says it. Her

clients are a little less compulsively loved—or perhaps
her concern has simply expanded beyond their narrow
range. She says the dinner parties are less frequent,
though Sue isn't yet closing the door on Barbra and
Candy when she leaves for the day. "I'm always available
for emergencies," she tells them, "but there's no more
of the dropping-in-and-spending-the-day thing." But if
it seems like Sue might lighten her load, the phones start
ringing again and the wife of the writer becomes, once
more, the agent—and, if she gets her way, the studio
head.

Having created some space for herself and her marriage, there is a Sue Mengers emerging that is distinctly
non-*glammmorous,* nonepigrammatic—a little more like
the studio head she so wants to be. "If it were all stripped
away," Sue can say now, "I could function. The point is
that all the success is like anything else . . . and what
bothered me when I was younger is not being able to
experience it. Now I've experienced it, and it's a lot
better than what I had: the riding the crosstown bus in
the morning to rush to your desk to start typing by nine
A.M. and just being able to grab a prune danish and a
container of coffee from the cart. But now," Sue Mengers says, looking away from the phones for a long moment, "now, having had the success and having Jean-
Claude, I could go back to the other." Especially if "the
other" could be Warner's or Columbia or Paramount.

STATUS ANXIETY: MENGERS AND THE MERGER
New York

On January 1, 1975, Sue Mengers's employers, Creative Management Associates, the world's third-largest

talent agency, merged with the world's second-largest agency, Marvin Josephson Associates (parent company to International Famous Agency; Robert J. Woolf Associates, a sports agency; Chasin-Park-Citron, an independent film talent agency; and Robert Keeshan Associates, syndicators of *Captain Kangaroo*). The resulting superagency, called International Creative Management, has 125 agents, bringing it almost up to William Morris's size. Morris, ICM's only rival, has 139 agents around the world.

Both IFA and CMA seem to have gotten a good deal. Marvin Josephson took over CMA at a bargain price: $6.75 million (less than its book value) plus $4 million in accounts receivable and a cash reserve of over $2 million.

Freddie Fields, president of CMA, for his part, walked away with $225,000 a year through the run of his contract (it has thirty-one months to go), $906,832 for his CMA stock, and the right to live in his $815,000 Beverly Hills home (purchased by CMA for him last year) for a bargain $15,000 a year. Then there's the CMA stock—marrying IFA has caused it to practically double, jumping from $3.25 to $6.10, a nice profit for anyone who bought the stock for less than its issue price of $7 a share.

The best of all possible worlds? For the top people and stockholders, sure. But not necessarily for the agents. The day after the merger was formally announced last November, Sue Mengers hopped a 747 to New York to have dinner with Paramount chairman Barry Diller. She was guarding her flanks.

Her fears weren't groundless. The rule of thumb in the industry was that CMA had movie stars and IFA had TV action (they put together most of the prime-time television-series deals). Each time a show that IFA packaged ran on a network, IFA grew about $12,000 richer from the licensing fee alone. An agent who handled a few of those shows brought in a lot of money—more, for instance, than an agent who handled mostly film stars. It's strictly business, nothing personal, and although packaging *Kojak* doesn't have quite the same glamor as putting together *What's Up, Doc?* (which Sue did), agent for agent, dollar for dollar, it's the TV agent who counts more. Unless you're talking about Sue Mengers, who not only kept her agency in the black but also wasn't about to take second billing to any TV department, thank you.

Another of Sue's worries was style. She knew that Marvin Josephson, her new boss, is the sort of executive who issues dress codes and keeps a close watch on expense accounts. And he does not, unlike Fields of CMA, believe in big salaries and contracts for agents. Of IFA's sixty-six agents, only three had contracts. As for salaries, few made close to six figures, no matter how big their billings were. Freddie Fields, who wears pale-blue Courrèges jeans, had a dozen of his fifty-nine agents under contract, six of them at more than $100,000 a year.

So the merger meant more to Sue than a mere change of stationery: It was a potential threat to everything she'd worked twenty years to achieve.

What she did about it last December, according to Mengers watchers, was spread word that she was getting restless. That she was ready, and able, to handle a position with real clout, like head of production for a major studio. Spread word she was talking to Diller. Said to Warner's president John Calley, "Why is Warner's the only company that hasn't approached me for a job?"

It was a standard agent's ploy—make 'em think they're missing a hot property. And it may have worked. Because, amid all the buzzing, Sue managed to renegotiate a new, three-year studio-size contract, upping her income from $140,000 to $175,000 a year.

THE NEW HOLLYWOOD HAS ARRIVED. HE'S ITALIAN.
(Dino De Laurentiis Conquers America)

D ino De Laurentiis came to New York to build "Dino-on-the-Hudson," but even with his brilliant and innovative financing structures and his most-favored relationship with Paramount Pictures, it wasn't long before he too was forced to migrate once again—to a $2.5-million home in Beverly Hills and the former Paramount offices on Canon Drive. His expand-in-all-directions enthusiasm and his string of American successes ended at about the time he moved his operation to Los Angeles. *Lipstick* was a disappointment, *Buffalo Bill and the Indians* only a mild critical success, and *King Kong,* his $26-million favorite, has not, industry insiders say, grossed its production costs yet. So far it's unclear whether Dino will forge ahead with *King Kong II.*

No matter. Dino is less an independent producer than a force of nature, a one-man studio. As it does with every strong figure who wanders into town, Hollywood glorifies De Laurentiis, marveling at his ability to sustain a year-long multimillion-dollar hype of *King Kong* while he produces Ingmar Bergman's first English-language film. That Dino might abandon *King of the Gypsies*—allegedly because his market researchers discovered that Americans weren't interested in gypsies—and postpone *Ragtime* to work on films about killer whales and hurricanes does nothing to strip the gloss from his image. In an industry in which production is cut by a third each year, the ability to get even a *Mandingo* produced is no small achievement. So while Dino may not be all that the Hollywood boosters claim him to be, he is certainly no garden-variety producer getting his comeuppance. His career, as I suggested in this piece, is a roller coaster—and one that can reliably be expected to quickly rise again.

"Let me explain you what happen. I-a *love* Fellini—he one of my best friend, I know him twenty years—he-a one of the few genius that exist in the world today. Fellini come to me and he say, 'Dino, I need eight million dollars to make *Casanova.*' I say, 'Okay, Fellini, let's spend eight million dollars, but let's shoot picture in English.' He say, 'I no can do, is *impossible* to make artistic picture in English.' I have to say, 'I sorry, Fellini—use a big star, a Bronson, a Redford—or I-a going to have to pass. No eight million dollars for Italian movie. Suicide.' "

Next. David Susskind, the Earl of WNEW, is being ushered out of the Italian Mediterranean office on the fifteenth floor of the Gulf + Western Building. Susskind has been *hondling* hard, trying to raise $5 million to bring Buffalo Bill to the musical screen. He has failed, he has (temporarily) blown the meeting. As he's being propelled out the walnut doors, Susskind tries to recoup: "You know, Mr. D., many people have told me that if I'd only been born Italian, I would be Dino De Laurentiis." His potential financier continues to close the door on Susskind. "That's-a nice, David, that's-a nice."

Next, Michael Winner and Norman Wexler. Next, the rushes of *Mandingo.* For Dino De Laurentiis—Rome's Duddy Kravitz, P. T. Barnum, and Medici-in-exile—has arrived in New York and is scoring, *beeg.*

Going Hollywood

With *Valachi Papers, Serpico,* and *Death Wish* causing lines around the block, De Laurentiis, fifty-five, has at least secured himself a place on the *Variety* charts, generating $92.5 million at the box office while wheeler-dealering in English "which no is very good." Not a bad record for any producer, but remarkable in that it's been only eighteen months since Dino settled into his Central Park South duplex and opened his thirty-man office at the G+W compound, a short stroll away.

How has he managed this overwhelming output while his competitors stand on the sidelines watching Dino's cash register seemingly fill to overflowing? "He's the ultimate shlocker," says one. "Dino has the fanciest financial arrangements ever. And the shadiest," a high-placed Paramount official confides. "He's the fastest-moving man in this town. The man is absolutely instinctual, I think he's one of the great hopes of the industry" —this from ICM power Sam Cohn. "The man who is considered the most important European producer? Who has the courage to close every-a thing and move to the United States and no-a speak English? He have to be crazy like me . . . I lie here and I wait and I look and I see and I try to learn. I never let up," De Laurentiis himself will explain.

It hasn't always been such a gold mine for the Italian David Selznick. If success is a circus, Dino's career reads like its roller coaster, looping through fame and disaster. "He never looks back who hasn't got something gainin' on himself," says a character in *Death Wish,* Dino's bonanza (gross to date: $35 million). And while Dino didn't write the script, he certainly applauded the line, since it applies just as neatly to his career. Sprung on the Italian cinema at seventeen as an actor, a refugee from his father's spaghetti factory in Naples, Dino quickly saw where the real money was: In the war years, with neo-

realismo features being shot in the streets, there was a shortage of producers. Dino followed Rossellini and De Sica out of the studios, watched them shoot *Open City* and *The Bicycle Thief,* building the war-raped countryside into artistic metaphor. Even in those days, Dino's deals were . . . original. Yes, he bottled tap water in Naples and sold it as seltzer of Capri, but more: Trying to raise money for his first project, a forgettable epic called *Pompieri Bijou,* the seventeen-year-old was forced to call on his banker. Dino recalls, "He say to me, 'O-a-kay, Dino De Laurentiis, if we are to give you two million lira, what is the guarantee to us?' So I say, 'Mr. Prococare'—I-a remember his name, Mr. Prococare—'look-a at my face. The guarantee I give you is my face. I am what you see. And this-a face that you see. My face.' And he-a say to me, 'That's-a first honest answer I-a get. I-a give you the two million lira.' " And that face? Thirty-eight years after its initial triumph, the stimulus of money and power keeps the De Laurentiis features animated and boyish, as bubbly as the waters he once bottled.

Apocryphal or not, Dino peppers his conversations with dumb-luck stories, explaining away his white-elephant Dinocitta studio complex (opened in 1965, closed five years and $100 million later) to focus on his new American empire, which will, in 1975 alone, place eight features in production, all personally supervised by De Laurentiis. His escapes from disaster don't interest him, only incessant *tummeling:* he has already produced five hundred movies, some memorable *(La Strada, Nights of Cabiria, Bitter Rice*—whose star, Silvana Mangano, became Mrs. Dino shortly after filming in 1948—*The Bible, Ulysses,* and *Romeo and Juliet),* others not so memorable *(Girls Marked Danger, Side Street Story, Waterloo, She Walk).* Actually, the list of forgettables goes on and on, understandable when *"Presenta por Dino De Laurentiis"* has meant an average of twenty features a year.

Yet Dino is ubiquitous, overseeing every aspect of his productions, making decisions with a lightning snap of the fingers. "No-a bureaucracy of American corporations a-telling Dino what to do, what to buy." He's up at six, reading scripts and calling a world filled with distributors, making the deals in the "foreign territories" for whatever Dino movie is coming off the production line that month. From six A.M. to long past midnight, seven days a week, Dino works "the way I cook, with a-love, always with love," trading on the success of his first "American-American" film, *Serpico,* to expand in all directions.

Dino simplifies his *modus operandi* by finding a successful source and mining it over and over. "It started with *The Valachi Papers,"* recalls Peter Maas, author of *Valachi, Serpico,* and Dino's newest project, *King of the Gypsies.* *"Valachi* was a big best-seller, yet there had been no movie sale. It turned out the studios were afraid of the Mafia, afraid to touch it. Remember, this was before *Godfather.* I couldn't believe it; nothing was happening. Then one day I got a call from California, someone was saying, 'There's a guy in my office called Dino De Laurentiis who wants to buy your book.' I think his original theory was that in buying *Valachi* he took the onus off the American studios. Nothing much happened until Charlie Bronson got into the film [*Valachi* made the million-dollar Bronson as big a star in the United States as he'd been in Europe], then it wound up doing all right [gross to date: $25 million]. So the next time I saw Dino, he said, 'What are you working on?' I told him it was a book about Serpico: 'It's about a cop.' At the time I'd just seen *Valachi* and I wasn't overwhelmed, so I wasn't trying to sell him. Dino said, 'Tell me in twenty-five words.' I said, 'I'll take fifty. It's about a courageous cop who's an Italian, in fact, whose parents probably grew up across from your parents' place in Naples." (Such was to be the rapport between the real-life Serpico and Dino that during the filming, the two held long conversations in Neapolitan dialect so thick that Dino's translators couldn't understand it.) "And that was it. Dino kept saying 'I want'; and sure enough, he closed a four-hundred-thousand-dollar deal by noon the next day—all on a twenty-two-page chapter. The book wasn't even finished. Any other independent producer would have had to wait for all kinds of bureaucratic okays and financing deals. Dino doesn't work that way; he says yes or no in five minutes."

And after the book was finished, was Dino pleased? "Well," says Maas, "I asked him if he'd read it once it was in galleys, and Dino said, 'You know, Peter, I-a start the book last-a night after supper—ask Silvana—and I stay up all night in bed, reading the book. Finally, as the sun was coming up, I finish it, and I walk over to the window and I look down at the park and I say, 'Bravo, Dino, bravo.' "

There were even more kudos when *Serpico,* combining the talents of Maas, De Laurentiis, Al Pacino, and last-minute addition Sidney Lumet (John Avildsen, director of *Joe,* had quit the picture in a dispute over locations with Marty Bregman, Pacino's manager and the film's line producer) raked in $25 million at the box office; with a possible four-wall rerelease, television series, and a scheduled TV series floating tantalizingly ahead, the dollars don't seem to be abating. And Dino's gang is getting just about all of them—even though Paramount released the picture in the United States and Canada and Columbia released it abroad.

Which leads to the De Laurentiis financial wizardry, the baroque method he uses to extract maximum money out of his product. Whereas a normal producer entering into a deal with a "major" will treat the studio—Warner's, Columbia, Paramount—as the banker, asking for financing in return for a hefty producer's fee (say $200,000) and 15–20 percent of the profits, Dino "work-a different way." His setup is called a gross deal. No one else gets this kind of deal, and Dino gets it only from Paramount, perhaps because of his longtime friendship with G+W czar Bludhorn, perhaps because, as an industry insider says, "For other studios to give Dino that deal would be a precedent-breaker, because what's happening is that the producer's getting paid back before the studio gets its piece of the pie, and that's something studios won't do if they want to stay in business." Unless, of course, they're doing business with De Laurentiis, who's had an unbroken string of hits (eight so far) in America, with only one release, *Crazy Joe,* that hasn't made it big (and Dino says that will ultimately break even).

Here's how Dino has made $92.5 million in a year and a half via the gross deal: Dino puts up the initial money —to buy the book, commission a screenplay, and hire a director—*before* he approaches a studio. Then he can say, "The budget of my movie is five million dollars. From you, I want only two million [plus a standard million for prints and advertising costs]. This gives your studio the right to distribute the movie in the U.S. and Canada only. You get the first three million dollars back." Then it becomes positively Byzantine, but the bottom line is that while the studio does indeed recoup its investment immediately, that is often the bulk of the money it will ever earn from the product.

Marie Brenner

Each picture is different, but Studio X will wind up usually with something like 65 percent of the second $3 million, then 60 percent of the next $3 million, until, when the gross hits $12 million, Dino is getting a 50–50 split of the earnings. As the picture escalates, the percentage shifts to Dino's favor, so conceivably, on a film generating $25 million in the U.S. and Canada, Dino will ultimately collect 75 percent of all the money coming in.

And that's only his domestic earnings. Which brings us to the real Dino forte: the foreign territories. Since he views himself as the United Nations of film, Dino (or one of his free-lance field men) will travel the globe, getting advances from each and every foreign territory (there are over fifty), making the same individual deal he got from Studio X, invariably retaining his enormous profit percentage. "Dino is the only producer who thinks of the United States as just another territory," a Walter Reade executive marvels. "Remember the United States is-a only 50 percent of the world," Dino says. "The rest is other foreign territories." That $2 million Dino left uncovered back when he was negotiating his $5-million deal with the studio? The foreign territories to the rescue, for by now, with Dino's product a proven commodity, advance money against foreign distribution is always there for the asking. So Dino's movies can be more or less financed in advance money or pledges even before the cameras start rolling.

But. "There's no way he can be getting all that foreign advance money, no producer can do that," one of his competitors insists. "He has to have some shady means of outside financing." "He's always a step ahead of the bill collectors," the Paramount higher-up offers. "Dino always gives the people who have percentages of his movies a phony address in Italy when it's time for them to collect their profits. That phony address will usually turn out to be an empty lot." True that Dino was slow to pay off shareholders in both *Serpico* and *Valachi,* but as Sam Cohn, who represents most of them, says, "We always get paid. If the checks come from an empty lot, who cares? They come."

Nice-a, as Dino would say, but *somebody* was left holding the bag when Dino packed his tents in the Italian night and abandoned his Dinocitta studio, erected exactly fifteen miles south of Rome soon after the government offered huge tax breaks to anyone who would develop southern Italy. And where was the tax-break border line? About one foot north of the spot where Dino drove the first stake of his Hollywood-on-the-Tiber, now a haunted Nathanael West vision of empty sound stages and unused buildings.

Dinocitta is in receivership, its mail forwarded to the distant G + W compound. When Dino speaks of that experience (the name itself is a pun on Italian super-studio Cinecitta), he is understandably distressed. "That is only mistake I make in my life. Because if I build Dinocitta in New York, it would be fantastic. Roma no is right town any more. Big overhead and big operation. Was the big mistake of my life. It was my dream to have big operating studio, biggest in the world, the most modern. I did. I did."

But Dino is nothing if not a survivor. Ten years ago, according to Leo Jaffe, chairman of Columbia Pictures, "Hollywood was ready to write Dino off. He'd made one flop after another, all at his half-empty studio. Dino retrenched. Changed his plans, starting smaller, building up his cash again with spaghetti westerns. The man is a dynamo."

Like all dynamos, Dino travels best alone. His attempts

at business marriages have both failed. Partnership with Carlo Ponti ended in 1957, when Dino wanted to go worldwide; the much-talked-about union with the Rizzoli publishing empire was never consummated. Having raked in big bucks with *Serpico* in 1973, Dino suddenly found himself with the capability to realize his ultimate dream: the building of Dino-on-the-Hudson.

Like many new immigrants, Dino is an American-chauvinist, serving up his own version of the Hollywood success story. "The American movie industry is number one in the world today. Number one. Let me explain point by point. All the momentum in the hands of the American producer. They-a copy the European art film of a generation ago and use. Look at *The Sting,* look at *Serpico. The Sting* look like it-a made in the streets, you understand what I mean. Number two is the whole Italian movie industry is down because of money, because of the economic situation, because it now take-a five million dollars to produce a movie." More: "Is an important point. The men at the top. Like Selznick, Louis Mayer—*like me.* These men *love-a* the movies. This is not always true in America. Movies have to be made by *one* man. Warner, Thalberg, Selznick—all the men who make-a the industry, is only one man."

De Laurentiis is one of the last of the best: the producer as *auteur.* "Let me explain you my philosophy of twenty years. If the picture is a flop, the responsibility is the producer's. One hundred percent the producer. The producer make-a the decision to select the story, to approve the script, to select the star, to approve the final cut, to see the ad, the publicity. If the picture is a flop, the *producer* make-a some wrong decision. But . . . if the picture is a success, then the producer should get the credit. No?"

How does this one man/one movie theory translate into practice? Dino-style, it means: Shoot only movies with strong story lines, hopefully based on blown-up incidents from recent events. Use a big star, regardless of cost. Hold endless story conferences with writers and directors until the first day of shooting, then step into a Godfather role, available for advice, visiting the set "only for-a social reason." Also, throw good money after good, recycling the ideas and talents of those who have already made money; keep the family together. So Peter Maas, Norman Wexler (who rewrote the screenplay of *Serpico*), Michael Winner (director of *Death Wish* and *Stone Killers*) and Charlie Bronson *(Stone Killers, Death Wish)* all have ongoing projects or future deals with De Laurentiis. And if one project should fall by the wayside, the cast is inter-changeable: The $10-million Ingmar Bergman *Merry Widow* planned for 1974 will now be directed by Michael Winner, King of the Shoot-'Em-Ups, who, Dino says, "has a different view" than the overly expensive Swedish master. More: *Last of the Mohicans,* first adapted by Harvard lit grad James Toback *(The Gambler),* will now be reworked for Bronson and the foreign territories by a writer closer to the B-movie market.

So there's very little fat on the De Laurentiis development list. Not that all of Dino's projects are tightly plotted, bone-crunching, violently commercial, Grade A shlock—only some of them are. "When I arrive in this country," says Dino, "I start to make the pictures three ways. I make television-style movies, like *Three Tough Guys.* I make Italian-American movie using American actors and Italian director; that was *Crazy Joe.* And I make an American-American movie: like *Serpico.* Like *Death Wish.*"

In standard Hollywood tradition, there's a move afoot

to have De Laurentiis declared a Hollywood soothsayer, a savant who need barely speak the language to make the industry fall before him. It fails to consider some key facts. Yes, *Serpico* was bought on an outline, but Maas had delivered—with *Valachi*—and how bad could a Peter Maas project about "a courageous cop of Neapolitan origin" be? Not very, especially when two other studios were bidding at the same time. *Death Wish,* which will, like *Serpico,* gross $25 million "in all the foreign territories," like *Serpico,* was bought for its strong story line. De Laurentiis saw it as a vigilante film, something juicy for the Winner-Bronson duo—*not,* as much of the media would have you believe, because Dino had his finger right on the pulse of neighborhood neurosis. Even Dino's close friends say that he was stunned by *Death Wish*'s success in "the U.S. territory," expecting the profits primarily from Bronson's following overseas. Then there's the eternal violence question, since "strong story line" means action-violence-suspense-gore, any way you slice it. "Is no more than a mirror of society," Dino protests. "The nature of society is violent, the nature of the film is violent."

Or, as most-favored director Michael Winner says, "Life is an incitement to riot." When he is pressed about his penchant for violent and sensational movies—his next features New York's criminals, out on bail, taking over the city's streets—Winner retaliates by hurling the interviewer's Sony across the room, making himself absolutely clear.

Winner aside, the quality of De Laurentiis productions is on the upswing, not that Dino ever thought he was offering up less than the best. But then, Dino is a man of contradictions. An elegant Northern Italian dish is served with Lawry's seasoned pepper at his table. Dino-

Going Hollywood

the-Enlightened-Despot is also Dino-the-Dutiful-Son; his eighty-seven-year-old mother is constantly on the squawk box from Rome, and Dino wears a black tie in perpetual mourning for his father. He keeps two accountants on the payroll, but numerous Leo statues around for good luck, and superstitiously avoids deal-making on Friday the thirteenth. Conversations about bringing Homer and Thomas Mann to the screen take place over coffee tables stacked, at home and in the office, with skin mags. The image of Dino in the *Crazy Joe* cutting room, demolishing every bit of footage that showed star Peter Boyle moving, "because he no-a walk right," goes hand in hand with Dino bestowing final cut on favored directors—something even Bob Evans won't give. And none of this strikes its protagonist as grand irony.

Whatever his antipasto theory of life, his creative development list (projects scheduled for production at some future date) reads like a computer printout of a producer's fantasy of what life is like behind studio doors. Here's just some of next year's product: *Three Days of the Condor,* by James Grady, starring Robert Redford, directed by Sydney Pollack *(They Shoot Horses, Don't They?)*—Dino's entry into the CIA spy-thriller market; *One Just Man,* adapted by Norman Wexler from the James Mills book—Dino's hand-picked *Death Wish* zygote. There's *Starstruck,* by veteran Ernest Tidyman, Dino's disaster film, to be directed by Dick Sarafian *(Vanishing Point).* And Dino's plum, the Peter Maas *King of the Gypsies* story, which he hopes a Fosse, Coppola, or Altman will direct. More: *The Great Brink's Robbery,* a six-hundred-page Noel Behns crime story. Then *Detroit Boogie, The Last Dogfight, Last of the Mohicans,* a *Death Wish* sequel . . . and this is just the development list. (Unlike the major studios, where "in development" is tantamount to saying "in the morgue," a project on Dino's development list is an almost guaranteed paper-to-screen proposition.) Before the cameras now—Dino divides his weekend time between "social visits" to the various locations —are *Mandingo,* a Richard Fleischer *(Tora! Tora! Tora!)* epic about slavery in the Old South (Dino on *Mandingo:* "This is going to be big controversial movie. I have big opening in New Orleans. I have big opening in Chicago. Then I-a make escape to Europe") and *Two Missionaries,* a Disney-style feature with Terence Hill and Bud Spencer, next year's Bronsons. (Dino favors numbers in titles; it's easier to sell the foreign territories with a simple peg.) The mogul's reaction to the work ahead? "Oh, my God, I-a get tired just-a looking." Then he pulls out a cigar—a number from Havana, smuggled out of Switzerland in a dummy wrapper—and lights it contentedly, twinkling at his prospects.

But De Laurentiis is no imperial Borgia belching orders with the demagoguery of a Harry Cohn or the abrasiveness of a Frank Yablans. "Even his enemies are charmed by him," says one of them, a competing producer. "Dino loves life," Peter Maas says. "The most popular producer around," begrudges another. Gia, his secretary for twenty-three years, swears that Dino's moods never change "even in the midst of crisis," and the thing is, it all seems to be true. After Dinocitta went into receivership, Dino kept the full staff—hundreds of people—on the payroll in Rome for an entire year, not because they were doing anything, but because he felt guilty about the studio's closing. Detail after detail: The De Laurentiis inner sanctum is always open, with Dino often calling out to wandering Paramount people, "Hey, come in here, let me give you hello!''

Underneath it all, Dino is clearly no Pollyanna. Embroiled in negotiation with a heated Susskind is a diabolical Dino: "Let me add one thing . . . uh . . . uh . . . what you say your first name is? Ah yes, David. Of course." Susskind is reduced to a more pliable mass. Reporters are invited to spend afternoons with Dino, when he is negotiating with American directors and writers, men who perhaps wouldn't yell quite so loudly with the media observing.

A lovable Machiavelli, then? Probably. An overextended monarch juggling scores of projects in the style of the Art Deco movie moguls he so admires? Absolutely. And worse yet for the competition, there's continuity: Nineteen-year-old Federico is already vice-president for television, and considering that Dino never misses a Dalton PTA meeting, there's always a possibility that one of his other children, or even grandchildren—he's moved many of them into his apartment building—will also be groomed to succeed him. "When I-a move into United States, I-a move *exactly* like a man starting his first job. Like I-a never make a movie before. Because if you make-a movie like you make-a movie in Italy, you never going to be a big success in the United States." The smart money says that he'll be around for a long while.

WHEN ARE WE GOING TO MAKE A PICTURE TOGETHER?
Lester Persky Comes of Age

The first time I saw Lester Persky . . . well, maybe I heard him first. It was at the party after the premiere of *Lucky Lady,* and even in that crowd of first-nighters at "21" you couldn't not hear his voice, a nasal tenor that endangers glass. He sat in prime position, holding court at what Suzy might describe as Table Number One. "Insecure café society," one observer called this group. They didn't look insecure to me. This very special minyan—Nan and Tommy Kempner, Kenneth J. Lane, Elsa Pereti, Maxime de la Falaise— surrounded the raconteur like a noose. They hung on his every word, as society folk will do to the newly rich: out of bemusement and pity, an overwhelming need to be entertained coupled with the desire to dine out on gossip and show-biz epiphanies for the next few nights. From where I stood, I had a good view of the man's face. He looked only too happy to oblige his tablemates. His mouth moved continuously, his head bobbed up and down. His open mouth revealed a surprising gap between his teeth; his lip was obscured by a thick mustache. He was almost bald. He seemed neither short nor tall, neither thin nor fat. His age was indeterminate. He was badly but expensively dressed.

One thing was clear: The man talked as if he thought

his electric monologue sprinkled with one-liners was the flame which drew these moths, and that if he should stop for only a moment, his table of socialites and column names would pull away, leaving him marooned in an ocean of white linen.

Then I observed an extraordinary scene. A tallish woman—an ex-model, it appeared—approached the table, strikingly dressed in something which looked like a Galanos, all jet-black with bugle beads. Her face was lit by clusters of diamonds on her ears, neck, and arms. She seemed pulled by some secret and mysterious plan. Warmly she kissed the air pockets over Table Number One's collective cheek. Then, mischief in her eyes, she turned on the man with the gap in his teeth.

"Do you have your tickets?" she demanded.

He seemed not to recognize her or see her smile. "Tickets? What tickets?"

"For this evening," came her answer, fast and cold.

I watched him fidget. Then he allowed himself a nervous grin. "Of course I have my tickets. Somewhere."

"Well, where are they? I *must* see them." Her voice was rising like the wind.

And so was his level of agitation. "Just a minute, I'll look for them. They're here. No, maybe they're downstairs. I . . . maybe my assistant has them." He fumbled in his breast pocket, patted his pants, too unnerved to meet the woman's stare. His complexion went from white to ashen, as the encounter stripped his status from raconteur to poseur. He looked like a Kansas City jeweler who had wandered by mistake into the April in Paris Ball.

"Don't tell us you *crashed,* darling," someone said.

Nan Kempner was in a state of shock.

He was on the razor's edge now, his table erupting

beneath him. Suddenly he took a closer look at his ac-
cuser. *"Betsy! Darleeeng!* I didn't recognize you!" he bur-
bled, then kissed the practical joker's cheek as the tension quickly faded into very obvious relief.

I let a moment pass.

"Who is that man?" I asked a young producer standing next to me.

"That's . . . *Persky."*

"Who?"

"Persky. You know." There was a dramatic pause.
"Lester Persky. The man who saved Hollywood."

Lester Persky, who graduated from Brooklyn's Eastern
District High School along with Mel Brooks ("He was the
class *schmendrick,* I was voted Most Likely to Succeed"),
has, since 1973, almost outdone his classmate. With
partner, Richard ("Please don't print 'Dick' ") Bright, he
has invested $30 million into twenty-two movies, includ-
ing *Shampoo, Bite the Bullet, Taxi Driver, Funny Lady, The
Wind and the Lion, The Front, Bound for Glory, Harry and
Walter Go to New York, Missouri Breaks, Summer Wishes, Winter Dreams, The Golden Voyage of Sinbad, Crazy Joe,* and *The
Last Detail.* They did not exactly "save" Hollywood, but
they did perhaps save Columbia Pictures, extending its
floundering corporate life for three years. They did save
their several dozen investors tens of millions of dollars
in tax write-offs and depreciations. Their record of pick-
ing box-office winners has been unmatched by any other
film financiers; an investor who started with Persky-
Bright in 1973 has, if he placed his money in the right
package of their films, received over 100 percent return
on his investment, one tremendous tax credit, and eventual ownership of a very lucrative asset. And for that
lucky investor there is, as Richard Bright explains it, "no

end in sight." This is not idle talk: The Persky-Bright investors own the rights and all of what would, in palmier days, have been Columbia Pictures' profits on *Shampoo, Funny Lady, The Front,* and *The Golden Voyage of Sinbad,* among others. The Persky-Bright Organization, in short, has become the movie studio's studio—not bad for a couple of shoestring investors who had $100,000 to spend a short three years ago.

Along the way, Persky and Bright have watched their competition—the legitimate tax lawyers and accounts who wanted their deals, and the not-so-legitimate "shelter mavens" who bought Italian westerns and showed them once, at night, on Forty-second Street—fade into obscurity, leaving them with a virtual monopoly and every studio but Fox and Universal begging them for deals. In the process, Lester Persky's new-found financial power has made him, at least on the East Coast, the columnists' darling. He says he's moved up from the D crowd to the A crowd. He says he's now "close friends" with Sidney and Gail and Warren and Jack and Lily and Paul and Joanne and Truman and Tennessee and Rudolf and Misha. He's been making a lot of money, but that, for Lester Persky, isn't the biggest thrill. What really counts is that Lester Persky has been having a lot of fun.

The next time I see Persky, he is in a limo barreling down Park Avenue on a steamy summer night. This time I am inside. So are Andy Warhol and Bianca Jagger, Fred Hughes, and the *Interview* magazine entourage. Persky fondles Bianca's knee, focused on a long monologue about her beauty. Suddenly, as the limo approaches the intersection of Fifty-seventh Street and Fifth Avenue, a piercing scream fills the back seat: *"Eyes right . . . it's Persky-Bright!"* Hollywood's most flamboyant film financier's eardrum-shattering rhyme hangs in the air. With his eyes on his office, Lester Persky looks like a happy child.

We are on our way to another movie opening, this time for *The Ritz*. Persky's spirits are unusually ebullient, probably because this is one of the season's few films he is not involved with and the word of mouth has been less than mixed. He poses for the photographers, locking his hand around Bianca's arm. He accosts Arnold Schwarzenegger in the lobby of the Four Seasons, his fingers slipping on the body-builder's oversized wrist. "Oh, Arnold, wait for me. Walk up the stairs with me, Arnold, for the photographers. I want to be with Mr. World in the pictures."

"I'm not Mr. World, I'm Mr. Universe." Schwarzenegger frowns.

"Oh, Arnold," Persky says when the bulbs stop flashing, "when are we going to make a picture together?"

Inside the Four Seasons there are wall-to-wall celebrities and sycophants. *The New York Times* will call this the party of the summer. Eight hundred first-nighters mingle while a band plays in the pool and Rita Moreno splashes through her songs. Amanda Burden wears a Ritz T-shirt. Others fight their way through the food line.

Lester Persky is oblivious to food. He won't sit down for a minute. "This is like a bar mitzvah!" he shrieks in his haste to glad-hand Kenneth J. Lane, Diana Vreeland, talent manager Allan Carr, and Warner Communications chairman Steve Ross. He tells Bella Abzug she doesn't need that hunk of chocolate cake she's about to attack. He corners reporters from the *Times* and *Women's Wear Daily* and fills their notebooks with Perskyisms, most of which, to no one's surprise, will wind up in print. He works the room with an insatiable energy, punctuating every conversation with "Oh, when are we going to make a picture together?" People seem happy to see him; Persky makes almost all of them laugh.

Then he spots Jon Peters glowering by the door.

"Oh, hello, I'm Lester Persky." He pushes a hand shaped like a small flattened Bartlett pear toward Barbra's boyfriend. "I don't believe we've met."

"Yeah?" Peters snarls. "What do you do?"

Persky's smile is baked on. "Not much. I invest in films."

Jon Peters doesn't get the irony. "You invest in films, huh? What kind of films?" he asks, as he starts to turn away.

Persky lets half a beat go by. "Well, let's see. Probably nothing you've heard of. Some features. Maybe you've heard of one called . . . *Funny Lady?*" His delivery would do Don Rickles proud.

Jon Peters does not take this very seriously. What he sees as Persky's put-on fills him with ennui. "You financed *Funny Lady,* huh?" he challenges. "How much did it cost?"

Persky blinks and mentally computes, effortlessly multiplying megadollars. "Well, let's seeee . . ." He drags that last syllable to Hollywood and back. "My company put in nine million dollars, then we got the banks to kick in another six."

For the first time, Jon Peters smiles and shoves his hand out to meet Persky's.

A month later, it looked as if Lester Persky's fun was about over. In September, after months of hearings, investigations, and witnesses testifying in Florida and Washington, the Senate finally acted on the legislation which the House had passed in 1975. The loopholes in the tax laws which had enabled tens of millions of dollars to finance dozens of major films were now officially closed. And Persky-Bright had had the rug pulled out from under them. Or almost had.

If, as Joan Didion has written, the deal is the true art form of Hollywood, the masters of this art are the tax shelter specialists. They are little understood—perhaps because they developed their virtuoso techniques for movie deals only recently, in the early 1970s. Among the pioneers of this art, Burton Kantor, a Chicago lawyer, and Richard Bright, a Kansas City cattle-feeding expert, more or less simultaneously cast their eyes westward and had a revelation: If buying assets and leasing the management rights in real estate and cattle could squeeze through the IRS tax-depreciation loophole, why not the movies?

Why not indeed? Kantor perfected a type of shelter called the "service-company partnership." All he needed was to gather together 25 percent of the money needed for a film; the other 75 percent came from several banks, which collected their money from box-office receipts, not Kantor's investors. The investors did better than the banks, in many cases; their 25 percent share of the production costs entitled them to 20 percent of the film's gross, beginning with the first dollar. Thus, for a Kantor deal like *The Great Gatsby,* an investor who pumped $100,000 into the film by now has received $567,000— the original investment plus $467,000. Roughly half that money pays off bank loans; the rest is taxable profit, with the first $100,000 investment written off.

Richard Bright's approach was equally ingenious. His "amortization deal" allowed an investor to buy a studio's piece of a movie that had already been completed. Again, the payments were small, no higher than 25 percent and sometimes as low as 5 percent. The investor could deduct depreciation for the movie based on its full cost. More, he could apply this depreciation to offset income from other sources, benefiting here from the 10-percent federal investment tax credit. Under this system, the investor has no ceiling on his possible profits. The package of films which Persky-Bright acquired that included *Shampoo, Breakout, Bite the Bullet,* and *Funny Lady,* and the unreleased *Seven Men at Daybreak* was sold to their investors in $160,000 units. Within a year every investor had earned back his money. With profits still coming in— especially from *Shampoo,* which carries every loser in the package—the investors' returns will ultimately be of *Fiddler on the Roof* proportions.

"What we did," Persky explains, "is duplicate for our company the same situation that the distributors had, only in reverse. All we did was put groups of pictures together in one company so that if any one picture hit, it would carry the losers. Since the losers very rarely lost a third of their cost and a success might do three hundred percent, one hit could pay for ten failures."

And the arbitrarily named packages Persky and Bright pulled together were not rich with losers. The Devon package included *Taxi Driver, The Man Who Would Be King, The Front, Gator, From Noon Till Three, Harry and Walter Go to New York* ("They forced that one on me," Persky says. "They told me I had to take that one to help them out"), and the unreleased *Sinbad and the Eye of the Tiger.* There were other packages: Exeter and Barclay. After prep schools? "After English towns," corrects Bright. Prep schools or English towns, those packages have generated $200 million in film rentals (box-office figure is about three times that amount). The IRS is auditing some of these packages ("Just a routine audit, I have a letter to prove it," Persky says), and in the opinion of several business types, few of them friendly to Persky-Bright, the old Persky-Bright shelters will probably be ruled clean. It's just that even clean deals can't be made any more.

"About a year ago I saw the handwriting on the wall," Persky says, "which is why we're now doing other things. That's why we're moving forward with venture capital and production deals." So, the worry about setting up these much-less-advantageous financial structures and these responsibility-heavy production deals notwithstanding, Lester Persky is still having fun.

The third time I see Persky, several weeks have passed. He has become, in the interim, a film producer. Film Financier, thanks to the Senate, is an identity he has discarded. It has not been a painful sloughing-off: Persky's first producer's credit will be on the film of *Equus.* So he does not look the worse for wear. Why should he? He is sitting at the Duck Joint, a New York Czech restaurant, with Miloš Forman, director of his second film project, *Hair.* Also at the table are Mick Jagger, Catherine Deneuve, Ara Gallant, and Appolonia.

Persky works on his second helping of dumplings while Jagger explains his own theory of filmgoing: Five minutes at the beginning and another five at the end are quite sufficient to figure out any movie. He searches for an example to illustrate the theory. He comes up with *Taxi Driver.* The table laughs as a unit; they know how much money Persky has made from *Taxi Driver.* Persky laughs too; this week *Taxi Driver* is holding steady near the top of the *Variety* charts.

"Well, Mick," retorts Persky, "I fell asleep in your last concert, too."

"Oh?" says Jagger. "What night did you come?"

"The opening night, óf course."

"Well, why'd you come to that one? That's always the worst, with all the *chi-chis.*" Jagger fairly spits the words out.

"Because that's the one you got me tickets for," Persky says, and falls silent.

He recovers as the conversation moves on to the traumas of celebrity. Each star has an it's-lonely-at-the-top story: Jagger and Deneuve describe the terror of being mobbed, Forman recounts the anguish of a festival audience turning hostile. And then it is Persky's turn.

His stream of unending dish has slowed to a trickle. He racks his memory, drops his voice. "Well, I was recognized once, too," he begins gamely.

His companions turn to him with interest. Persky's face is not exactly head-of-the-coin material; his name is hardly a household word. "Yes, I was in London," Persky says, gathering strength. "In a taxi. The cabdriver turned to me and said, 'Aren't you the guy who was in *Heat?*' "

Everyone but the storyteller cracks up. The loudmouth producer Persky played in that Warhol film is clearly a role he feels ambivalent about. "That movie's going to follow me to my grave," he says, by way of a punch line.

It is after midnight, and the energy levels are flagging. But not Persky's. "Let's go to Elaine's. Let's go to Elaine's for a drink," he cries. "Mick. Milosh. Who's up for Elaine's?"

Jagger seals his rejection. "Oh, Lester, it's just another friggin' restaurant."

So we go to Regine's. Close to two in the morning, Lester Persky sits at a long table under the slivers of mirrored glass. He is in deep ecstasy. He is surrounded by stars, and Warren Beatty has just paged him to the phone. He returns to the table with a news flash: Warren is over at the Plaza working on the Howard Hughes script. He may join us later. The news excites only Persky. The group is more concerned with Dom Perignon and pastries. A William Morris agent wanders over. He is given the freeze. Yasmin Aga Khan drops by. She is not given the freeze. Persky says to Catherine Deneuve, "Oh, *Cathereeene,* when are we going to make a picture together?" Not right away, it seems.

Persky knocks back a glass of champagne. He talks about his good friends Warren and Jack. He is incredulous that Nicholson is suing *Missouri Breaks* producer Elliott Kastner for a million that Nicholson alleges was withheld from his earnings percentages. "But that has nothing to do with me," Persky amends, anxious to be good friends always with his good friends. That they are not always so flattering about their good friend does not matter; reality is a factor often suspended when one is ruled by star-struck visions. "If Lester were half as good as his hype, he'd be David O. Selznick and Monroe Stahr," a Good Friend will say.

At two thirty, Persky is still talking. "Do you realize that after everything is paid back, Dick Bright and I are splitting *ten million dollars?"* I look at Persky, astonished. After a torrent of words about Warren and Jack and Candy and Sidney and *Equus* and *Hair,* will Persky blurt out everything? I wait to hear that this remark is off the record. But Persky goes on.

Across the table, Mick Jagger calls for the bill. We have consumed, by my count, two bottles of champagne and some pastries, a gift from Regine. Jagger lays three crisp hundred-dollar bills on the table and exits.

Persky looks at me. "That's the way stars behave," he announces.

Marie Brenner

The first and only time I see Richard Bright, he is in his office, which is half the size of his partner's and is decorated only with a picture of his wife. He does not want to be interviewed here; he seems to fear that Persky will pop in and be so helpful that this infrequent encounter with an interviewer might as well not take place. Bright suggests a quiet drink around the corner in the Drake bar. I have to lean in: His voice is practically a well-modulated whisper, as hushed as his suit. Everything about him is toned down; he looks slight, seems younger than his forty years. There is an element of an undefinable Scarsdale-gone-to-prep-school patina in his manner.

But there is palpable tension in his tone as he describes how he and his partner could not have less in common. Perhaps this is because some of the jokes Persky makes at his expense ("My partner's away for three months, but you know my partner, even when he's here, he's away" and "My partner Dick Bright doesn't look very bright") have floated back to him. Being the butt of a man who used to think up jingles for tuck tape and press-on nail polish is not the role that Bright implies a Hotchkiss and Wharton education has groomed him to play. That seems to annoy Bright, but what really galls him, perhaps why he has consented to talk to someone who doesn't represent the financial press, seems to be Persky's continual use of the first person singular instead of the plural.

"Lester can say anything he wants about his own role as a 'creative producer' on *Equus* and *Hair,*" Bright says, "but not on the financial aspects of our company. And it seems like that's all I've been reading about lately."

But what about that $10 million that's getting split down the middle?

Bright hesitates, unsure which $10 million I mean. Then he senses Persky's let it out of the hat again. "I was brought up to believe that when you have a good deal, you keep quiet about it," he says stiffly, and closes the subject.

The next question, of course, is how these opposite souls became partners. Bright warms slightly, outlining the concept of film amortization purchases. "Oh, how did I meet *Lester?* Someone brought him to me. I believe Lester was . . . semiretired at the time. It was clear that he and I came from . . . different backgrounds." Bright clears his throat. "Lester had produced *Boom!* and some other film [*Fortune in Men's Eyes*]. Neither was successful, yet he offered me some knowledge of the contractual realities of this very treacherous business, a business I wasn't used to dealing in. Frankly, I needed someone who could negotiate in the swamp of Hollywood and leave me to the strictly financial aspects."

Like his partner, Bright bristles when the subject of tax shelters comes up. "If we were just interested in tax shelters, we would have spent the last three years acquiring spaghetti films like a lot of other people who are now out of business." How did he strike upon the idea of buying a studio's assets? "I'd been in the venture-capital business for fifteen years with Oppenheimer Industries, Inc. [a major cattle-feeding financier], and I came across Burton Kantor's production-service deals. Burt was like a contractor in the construction industry with these movie deals. I saw some basic tax problems with those kinds of deals. I thought, 'Wouldn't a surer way to do business be to buy the building *after* it's completed, rather than build the building for someone else?' "

The buildings Bright sought to buy were all over at Columbia Pictures. Knowing enough to want to buy them is one thing; knowing that they were for sale is quite another. "Oh, I grew up down the block from Stanley Schneider," Bright says airily. "I kept informed." In 1973, the Schneider family owned a large amount of the stock of Columbia Pictures. Given that the film business tends to be incestuous, it seems at least an irrefutable irony that Lester Persky—who takes credit for Persky-Bright's success, who "knows the world"—didn't know the right people at the right time. And Richard Bright, who comes, as Persky says, "from cattle," did.

Burton Marcus, the former vice-president and general counsel of Columbia Pictures, gives the impression that Columbia Pictures, and his charity, have been carrying the both of them. "You have to remember that a lot of hustlers were coming to Columbia with tax-shelter schemes in 1973. Lester was just another one of them, and not, at that point, the one with the best track record."

The situation was indeed grave for Columbia in 1973, perhaps even terminal. In June, the corporate bank debt had risen to $163 million and equity had bottomed out near $6 million to $8 million. The big Columbia pictures were *Oklahoma Crude, Castle Keep,* and *Lost Horizon;* the write-offs on these pictures alone would assure the company of tax losses for years to come. Taxes, however, were far from executive minds. The problem was the decided absence of income. Keeping secretaries in salaries and carbon paper was suddenly a challenge, to say nothing of the $15 million a year that a studio like Columbia needs to stay in production.

"I simply had to find a money market," Marcus says with noble restraint. So, with the help of his computers, he devised a scheme to enable Columbia to give away a certain amount of potential profit while offsetting the risk of financing its movies. "These deals were nothing new," Marcus adds. "The concept was no different than buying a piece of real estate and only putting ten percent down." He fudges a little here. What was new was the spectacle of a studio selling a major part of what would ordinarily be its future equity.

Persky-Bright's big break came when Columbia assembled an enormous package that Persky-Bright later called "Vista," which included almost every good film the studio planned to release in 1974–75: *Funny Lady, Shampoo, Breakout,* and *The Fortune.* Columbia wanted to sell, Persky-Bright wanted to buy. Unfortunately, Columbia wanted $29 million, with $7 million as the down payment. More unfortunately, Columbia was also offering the package to film financier John Heyman. Lester Persky, the most tenacious of a tenacious bunch of players, was waiting in the wings. But he had a serious reservation: He didn't want *The Fortune.*

"With *The Fortune,* the deal was too rich," Persky says.

The Persky-Bright luck was still running; Columbia remained convinced up to opening day that *The Fortune,* with Nicholson and Beatty and Mike Nichols as the director, would be their big winner. Whereas *Shampoo* was thought to be a dog; Beatty's producing deal called for him to retain a large percentage of the gross. "It'll never make more than six million," a Columbia executive commented about *Shampoo.* So Columbia held on to *The Fortune* and sold the copyright on *Shampoo* and the others to Persky-Bright. *Shampoo*'s gross will probably hit over $100 million. *The Fortune* bombed. And in that one corporate decision lay the next stage of Lester Persky's advancement.

"Lester's always wanted to be a producer," says Burton Marcus. "It must really gall him that he's only been successful as a money man," another executive conjectures. "Nobody in Hollywood takes his producing claims seriously," insists a producer whose film made money for Persky-Bright. "People are glad his money's around. It's helped a lot of movies get made. But most of the producers and filmmakers will tell you the same thing: We don't really know him. All I know is that he's a guy who comes around, flatters you, and kisses you a lot. He's relatively harmless. He has no power. He's neither your partner nor does he represent the studio in any way. Usually the squabbles are between the filmmakers if one starts claiming credit he's not entitled to, but with Lester it's different. He's in New York, he comes from another world. He's annoying, but he's more like some kind of gnat. The only way he comes in are with the financial guys who show him what amounts to the fall line. He says, 'I'll take one of those or two of these.' "

The fourth time I see Lester Persky, he is silent, but only because he is wolfing down a hamburger at a neon-lit coffee shop at Fifty-ninth and Third. The burger is the hors d'oeuvre; *Equus* is the main course. Persky speed-raps for an hour, recreating the history of this deal. Soon he will be off to Canada to be with Sidney Lumet and his all-star cast and crew. Persky pauses only to grab a toothpick and search for hidden burger bits. "Darling, forget this 'Won Ton Ton who saved Hollywood' business. I'm the man who saved Hollywood."

And he hopes that Hollywood will return the favor. Three times in a month, he will share his plan with me: "My major time now is setting up a vehicle for my company, Persky-Bright, to have a production company so we can acquire properties and produce them, with me as the actual producer." So far his creative choices are curious: the seven-character *Equus,* with Richard Burton and Peter Firth, and the 1960s throwback *Hair,* which hasn't found a viable approach in five years with several producers. Clearly Persky is drawn to the theater, and the respectability and dignity it confers. But in his efforts to make plays as profitable as films, he finds himself deeply mired in the Hollywood swamp. This does not trouble Lester Persky. He has Miloš Forman contracted to direct. Forman's last film, *Cuckoo's Nest,* broke $100 million and that had been kicking around for a long time too. He has Sidney Lumet directing *Equus,* and Miloš Forman contracted to direct *Hair.*

The last time I see Lester Persky, he is completing his *rite de passage.* I am waiting for the full-fledged producer in the two-story studio outside of Toronto while he talks on the phone to New York. This gives me time to examine my surroundings and determine that this studio could pass for a suburban dental complex. I take refuge in Richard Burton's trailer and idly ask him to describe his producer.

"Ah, you mean Persky." Burton builds slowly. "Really, I hardly know the man. He greeted me at the airport when I arrived and I've hardly seen him since. Oh, except when the press people were here on some junket. Then he spent a lot of time kissing me in front of them, telling me how wonderful I was."

A few hours later, Persky is talking about Richard Burton: "He's marvelous. A good friend. Known him for years. The first night we were here we stayed up till God knows how late reciting Welsh poetry to each other."

Persky emerges from his office, and he goes into high gear, carrying on like a backstage Johnny who has slipped through the stage door and been made welcome.

He's betting *Equus* will gross $20 million—which, coincidentally, is how much venture capital he and Bright are hunting for. Unless some Wall Streeters convince them to go public first. And more immediately, isn't it fabulous that Sidney is two full days ahead of schedule. And Burton isn't drinking. And everyone is getting along.

All day long, Persky is this way: lovable, self-dramatizing, charming, and manipulative. Out on the producer's limb in the Canadian wilderness, he seems to feel exposed, burdened with fantasies like garish Vuitton luggage he should have left behind. He's too ebullient even for a New York opening, too quick to jump on the defensive, as if he's outgrown the old Persky without having a convenient mask handy for the new one.

"Do you realize all the things that could have gone wrong with this production?" he asks, grabbing at my coat sleeve. "Do you realize that if I hadn't suggested Burton and been the one to work with Sidney and said that Elliott Kastner [technically the co-producer] shouldn't be on the set, that the atmosphere around here wouldn't be as nearly as calm as it is?"

For once he is not making a joke; in the center of his own fever, Persky cannot see that he is the ragged, turbulent element here. He is no Bob Evans, finessing the main chance. It is thirty degrees out, but the reason Persky wears no coat is not to make an impression, but because his anxiety is sufficient heat. Can he fail here and keep the Hampshire House penthouse he's just bought from Atlantic Records mogul Jerry Wexler? Can *Equus* get killed by the critics and Persky continue to be recognized by Elaine? Who is this Persky, even to himself?

My last image of Lester Persky is of the still-successful producer. He is walking back toward his beloved set. He is completely alone. But he is very much in motion.

RUMBLINGS
FROM NIRVANA:
THE GOLDEN DOOR

"**H**ere at The Fountains we create a womb environment, a secure and protected place. Here women find respite from the pressures of their outside lives. But we have a larger purpose, too. Our real goal is to lead women to other, more meaningful fountains."—Sylvia Wallace, *The Fountains*

It wasn't like that at all, at least not on the first night. A womb? Women being led to meaningful fountains? This was more like a funeral. No one had anything to say. Twenty-seven women, arranged like cold cuts in the ersatz Japanese dining room—you'd think they'd be falling all over one another with tales of their mutual physical and emotional disrepair. It wasn't like they were novices at the spa game. On this particular week in May, half of the Golden Door's guests were returnees. They knew the routine; some even knew one another from other years, even other spas. Wilamette Day and Nancy Bogdanovich hadn't seen each other since high school forty years earlier in Pasadena; they'd had a stunned reunion only hours before this very silent dinner. And all of the guests —new and old, adolescents and grandmothers, celebrities and housewives—shared one obvious, extraordinary bond: As they polished off the last of the consommé-soaked chicken that the Golden Door calls Yosenabe, the

Golden Door bookkeeper was getting ready to deposit twenty-seven checks for $1,200 each (plus $200 in tips). To spend that much for six and a half days of weight reduction (average loss: five pounds) in a resort separated by more than distance from men and *not* gush with the girls from minute one was not *de rigueur* spa etiquette.

The few animate clusters at the far ends of the T-shaped table were women who had arrived together. The young wife of the heir to America's largest stocking fortune sat with her best friend, the equally youthful wife of a North Carolina textile-mill owner ("a small one," she explained). The Texas Troika: two middle-aged wives whose husbands controlled a Texas oil company ("a private one," the older noted), dragging along one daughter-in-law, whose husband was not in the oil business ("Our husbands decided early that none of the children would be allowed in," sniffed the other). A seventy-year-old mother brought her forty-five-year-old daughter. "I came to gain weight and keep Mama company," she said, straight-faced. There were women of distinction, some with friends: Liz Carpenter with Antoinette (Mrs. Mark) Hatfield, Mrs. Starkist Tuna back for her seventeenth visit, greeted by the three-inch plaster-of-paris statue of Charley Tuna that the Door keeps as her special place card. Lady Caroline-in-Exile, the twenty-year-old daughter of a London financier, was back for her third visit in a year, to shake seven extra pounds before joining her family in the south of France; her companion was a nine-carat, pear-shaped diamond, "a gift from Daddy." Even the Lockheed shift worker in the polyester pants suit who'd saved for two years to come to the Door wasn't one of a kind; there was at least one California housewife whose children had given her a week here as their collective Christmas present.

So this was, on the surface, a heterogeneous group of women who might reasonably be expected to view Deborah Mazzanti's $3.2-million Japanese inn as the greatest all-female treat since summer camp—only here, along with the seven A.M. hikes and four-raspberry breakfasts, they offer foot massages and "DaVinci exercise classes" conducted to Smokey Robinson. But as the women nibbled on the low-calorie chicken, not even banalities about the regime broke the silence; they were too busy checking each other out to speak.

Or perhaps it was that the old-timers were noting the changes with cold horror—the "new" Golden Door, opened in August of last year on an Escondido hillside, does feature alarming signs of creeping commercialism. Two Louis XIV–interiored mobile units have been permanently installed near the kitchen, besmirching the harmony of the rooms set by the azalea gardens. And the boutique plunked in the middle of Courtyard #2—"The Bell Garden"—dispenses merchandise that pales once it leaves Rodeo Drive. The human factor is equally akilter at the new Door. The greeter who welcomed this group was decidedly plumpish; though she would be inoffensive at the Door's sister spa in Baja California, Rancho La Puerta. Here her cheeriness strikes a stridently false note. Fat on the staff? How could Deborah—as she is known to all—expect to keep the loyalty of weight-conscious regulars like Leigh Taylor-Young, Kim Novak, Barbra Streisand, Bess Myerson, Debbie Reynolds, and Barbara Howar with a size fifteen at the gates?

Over dinner, the silent guests encountered another disarming "new" Door phenomenon: the Michel crisis. The Golden Door's renowned chef, Michel Corrado ("the old Michel"), had wantonly divulged his literary plans to Kitty Kelley. That interview was mass-marketed in her book, *Glamour Spas*. "I will call my book *The Society*

Stud," Michel had bragged. "It will make more money than *The Happy Hooker.*" Corrado was replaced by Michel Stroot ("the new Michel"), who limits his extracurricular activities to dozens of daily phone calls to his girlfriend. And she lives just down the road. Only this week even the new Michel was off, and the forty-calorie mousse tasted distressingly like chocolate chalk. Women began making odd faces as they sampled dessert. Then Fanny, the physical therapist, and the evening's hostess, asked her charges to stand up and introduce themselves. Dessert suddenly became a major attraction.

"I'm Liz Carpenter," a voice boomed from the end of the table. "I don't know what I can tell you all except that I've been active in politics all my life—and that's been a long time—and I'm proud to say I'm a dyed-in-the-wool Democrat and I will continue to be." For emphasis, she pounded the table. A smattering of nervous laughter, the first group response of the week. Then a tiny figure rose from the table, mousse in hand. Not looking back, she skulked out of the dining room. "I think I've offended someone," Liz Carpenter said.

The offended matriarch turned out to be the loyal ex-wife of a defeated North Carolina gubernatorial candidate. Her exit rendered the rest of the introductory remarks minimal: name, number of children, home town. Clearly, some veterans whispered, this might be a week to keep a low profile, maybe even follow Dyan Cannon's Golden Door routine—hide out in a raw-silk-and-pastel bedroom, subsisting on infinitesimal amounts of carrot and celery juice. But no one did this. Not with that media-praised, friend-recommended Golden Door routine beginning at six forty-five the next morning.

Make that half past six, when it's time to "wake up and

weigh in." Then the six forty-five hike up the mountain. Collapse again under a silk bedspread an hour later until a tray comes, bearing breakfast (no more than a sliver of melon, or four berries, and sometimes a single egg), the Los Angeles *Times,* and a pastel daily schedule shaped like a fan. A Tibetan gong interrupts this nirvana, its hollow thud penetrating the three courtyards, two swimming pools, two Japanese bathhouses, three gyms, and various beauty rooms, lounges, and tennis court—it's time to "warm up."

By ten thirty, you are plenty warm. You are also stretched, flexed, and pulled, having endured two DaVinci fifty-minute sessions in which the mind has been taught to make the body "a perfect circle." The over-fifty's—about half of this group—have had a little trouble fathoming the significance of these gravitational calisthenics; somehow, a Japanese inn amid a forest of cypress trees doesn't quite go with John Sebastian blasting the theme from *Welcome Back, Kotter* through giant speakers.

But the first-day routine is designed to turn even the most resistant grandmother into a Golden Door zealot: the menu is a "Virtue-Making Juice Fast," guaranteed to melt off three pounds in twenty-four hours. It is good that everyone is told about this attraction; the orgy of narcissism the juice fast inaugurates stifles what would otherwise be massive confusion—the group has been splintered into advanced, intermediate, and beginner groups, although this is comprehended only by returnees and the girls who make up the schedule fans. As it is, isolated women look too perplexed to ask why one group has six hours of gym-and-swimming, another has dance-and-DaVinci, and a third is to spend most of its day under the herbal wrap. The Golden twenty-seven meet only at drink-time—for almond milk, a blend which, depending who's on blender duty, can taste either like a banana milkshake or Kaopectate-on-the-rocks. With Michel away, it tends toward the latter. This does not stop the virtue-makers from wolfing it down with silver demitasse spoons.

Euphoria! Visions of maybe-just-maybe being able to lose those ten pounds in six days caress us like the sun. The absurdity of these fantasies does not hit the "advanced group" until midway through the pelvic tilt in the post–almond milk DaVinci class. We thrust higher and higher, smalls of our backs press-press-pressing up to the ceiling. Our abdomens practically brush the light fixtures; so anxious are we for these tilts to be perfect that the voice of Ginger, the exercise teacher, seems to be directed toward some other class. "Higher! Higher! Higher!" she yells over the Rolling Stones. "Work on your *squeeeeezzzes!*"

Only then does one begin to check out the Felliniesque montage: a baker's dozen of women working on vaginal contractions on the flat-weave carpeted studio. Half of them wear the shapeless, fading Golden Door jogging suits; half suffer in the Door-provided pink Banlon Bermuda shorts and carnation T-shirts that can't look like a Theodore's T no matter how skinny you are. By this time, some of the group has been through "Beauty"—their hair has been doused with the mud-thick coconut-avocado oil that will remain on all week. Thankfully, the results are tied back with neon-colored yarn. Mrs. Starkist Tuna looks as silly as the Lockheed worker. "I almost forgot my hair was blond," novelist Lois Wyse recalls.

The point of this purposeful shlumpiness is far from casual: The Golden Door does seek to level its clientele into an egalitarian unit. But even on the first day of exercises, it's almost too late for that to happen; having survived the mutual checking-her-out dinner, we're now waiting to latch on to our best-friend-for-a-week. And mostly we're wondering when the $1,400 worth of pampering begins. The promotional literature may promise "a womb of expensive serenity" and the reams of gushing articles by the journalists whom the Door welcomes with freebies really do make the unsuspecting believe that handmaidens are ready to whisk away soiled towels the moment they drop from an exercise-fatigued hand to the parquet floor. None of this, however, is in evidence. It does not appear as the week wears on, either. "I didn't even have fresh soap in my bathroom the last two days," a Dallas art dealer says instead of good-bye.

Not that anyone is being deprived. Not when they're sitting by the turquoise swimming pool overlooking Southern California hills, having midday gazpacho with a thimbleful of sunflower seeds served from a silver tea cart. But here the subtle difference between those-in-the-know and the others is becoming less subtle; the veterans always request "luncheon by the pool." Better to stick close to the chaise longue and get some sun in peace than get trapped in the dining room next to someone who's hungry for friendship. Someone like Phyllis. The question about Phyllis—a loud-mouthed and overweight peroxide blonde—is not what she's about, but why she's at the Door at all. For the tacit promise, the unspoken lure of the Golden Door, is that the yentas will be at Murietta Hot Springs. This one slipped through. And she made her presence felt. "I'm Phyllis, from Phyllis's House of Jewels . . . in Baltimore?" she'd shared that first night, looking around the room to see if her store provoked a flicker of recognition. It didn't. That upset her. And her upset grew: House of Jewels was moved from one terraced Camellia Garden room to another; Mrs. Stocking Fortune was socked into her old suite. By the next morning, she was close to frantic. "I've been missing a lot of my phone calls," she complained on the hike. She turned to Mrs. Stocking Fortune. "Have you been getting them?" Mrs. Stocking Fortune shook her head. "Well, what about my flower arrangements? Have you seen my flowers? My son said he sent them. Are you sure you haven't seen them?"

By behaving in this hostile-aggressive, very un–Golden Door way, the House of Jewels has set in motion the dynamic that will coalesce at least a third of this week's group: She has mobilized them into a clique that opposes her; she has given them something to talk about besides carrot sticks and face lifts, something nonpersonal, noncommitting. House of Jewels has, in fact, provided the first clue to the larger dynamic that hides behind the allure of a $1,400 week at the Golden Door. A better body, a purified state of mind, improved health and vitality—yes, those are the surface benefits the Door offers. But the larger ethic behind those siren calls is more powerful for the twenty-seven women who have either survived and/or ignored the feminist revolution. Theirs is a more important balm: letting one's hair down with the girls, not feeling guilty about indulging in anachronistic female behavior. Ladies' lunches. Gym classes. Conversations about laugh lines and saddle bags around the hips. Now that's heaven. So the secret of the Golden Door's drawing power is that here a smallish group of like-minded women can rediscover the tacky camaraderie of endless cigarettes-and-coffee of the sorority house. Life was such fun then, because we were free to be shallow. Free to talk about clothes, boys, cellulite, lip gloss, diets, and other women . . . like Phyllis.

Afternoon. This is when low-grade anxiety sets in, fueled by the winding down of the morning's frenzied exercises. Twenty-seven paths cross as we trudge in our white plastic Golden Door scuffies across the redwood walkways to the beauty rooms where feet are massaged, pores are cleaned, eye shadow is evenly applied, legs are waxed, and baby oil is kneaded into semi-stretched thighs. "When you're physically tired, you get time for your mind to come through," Deborah Mazzanti insists.

Sometimes one hears other things. Like the voice of the masseuse giving a private hour's massage in the privacy of a bedroom: "You know, I worked on both Miss Streisand and her agent. That blonde lady, Miss Mengers? Miss Streisand was real nice, but that Miss Mengers! On the phone, all the time . . . she kept the phone by the massage table and she was always yelling or swearing at somebody. Poor Miss Streisand—Miss Mengers wouldn't let her out of her sight. And if one of the other guests started to talk to Miss Streisand in the sauna, she'd say, 'Come on, Barbra, we've got to go *right now!*' How did Miss Streisand do on her diet? *Real good.* But Miss Mengers, she had candy all over her room, and I heard she never went to exercise class." A few gossip sessions like these as the masseuse works on one's inert body, and another of the always-operative attractions of the Golden Door becomes apparent—hang around here or at the Greenhouse or Maine Chance, and even a Lockheed shift worker can pick up a few choice nuggets of gossip about the very rich and famous.

Kim Novak, for example, never weighs in. Once her pet billy goat rammed a hole in her bathroom door (the new spa allows no pets). Two years ago, Leigh Taylor-Young came for eight weeks, had an affair with "the old Michel"—and lost not a pound. The girl who gave me facials reported that Bill Blass asked for (and got) his chest hair dyed. Mr. America works out with the men during the twice-a-year men's weeks. During the Watergate hearings, Mrs. H. R. Haldeman demanded that the television in the lounge be turned off. Barbra Streisand sat next to Mrs. Dayton's Department Stores in lip-and-eye class. "I've never felt so poor in my life," La Streisand said.

The spa set has little to feed on except this minor gossip, and more than just the guests take to it like protein injections. The Mexican driver who chauffeurs guests to the airport announced to two women, "Martha Raye was just here." The Dallas art dealer in the back seat rose to the bait: "How does she look?" "Old," he replied. Once we're beyond the juice fast and into such delights as Pineapple Surprise for cocktails and two-hundred-calorie dinners of Chicken Sauté Sukiyaki and Broccoli Vapeur, even the frailest of these nuggets of dish are traded like diamonds. There's really nothing else to do.

Twenty-seven ladies who should know better are reduced to racing for their place cards the instant the Tibetan gong rings at seven o'clock. In the dining room, cliques are forming now. A smokers' table is established. Women cling to one another like suitors, dreading the night and its unbroken expanse of boredom.

For $1,400, there really ought to be more happening at night than a session in the Jacuzzi ("The Japanese Family Tub") with the House of Jewels and the Texas Troika for company. Stories about Lucy Johnson's eight-foot-high, butterfly-decaled baby-blue garbage cans pall after an hour or so. The occasional flower-arranging class or decade-old feature film is not enough to convince anyone that this is the S.S. *France* of spas. Nowhere do Mazzanti's cost-cutting economies show more acutely than in those nonorganized nights, which, in memory, seem more vivid than the marathon activity of the days. But soon the days begin to melt into one another as well, with only a few bumps on the road to what the literature calls "the innermost world of being."

No one thought the first bump would hit Candy, the Multiple Sclerosis fundraiser from Denver. But there she was, thinner by eight pounds—which, thanks to the juice fast, she lost in a single day—and in an absolute crying jag. Right in the middle of the hip rolls, with her four-foot countergravity pole counterlevitating her head, Candy started to sob. The women in the front rows started to turn around as her hysteria drowned out Tom Jones singing "Candy Man." "I don't want to be left behind," she shrieked, as her energy sank below sea level and her nerve endings turned into wet Kleenex. She was quickly shuttled out by the pool, where bread and honey and bacon and eggs were shoveled down her throat. "Low blood sugar," an exercise girl explained. "It sometimes happens after the juice fast." Another volunteered, "The problem with this place isn't the guests, it's the management. How many spas have no medical supervision whatsoever? In Europe this is unheard of."

Mazzanti gets around this sticky situation by catering to the faddists, indulging their eccentricities. For days, Lady Caroline drank nothing but hot water and lemon juice. Candy, the Multiple Sclerosis fundraiser, was back on her juice fast three days after her collapse; the staff was noticeably silent about the intelligence of this decision. Not that there was really a voice of authority around to deliver a verdict for or against. The Door's former manager, Anne Marie Benstrom, had long since left to marry the president of Flying Tigers Airlines, Bob Prescott, whom she'd met during men's week; she now runs the Ashram, just north of Malibu. The new manager, Margaret Logan, wasn't scheduled to start until July. And where was spa-owner Mazzanti? Overseeing Rancho La Puerta in Tecate, Mexico, some said. Others suggested she was in San Diego, looking after her umbrella company, Fitness Resorts, Inc. But no, Deborah was really on the East Coast, accepting yet another award: California Small Businesswoman of the Year.

She's far from that. At fifty-four, the slightly plumpish graying Mazzanti is the country's spa-owner nonpareil, a tireless self-promoter who's managed to parlay a Brooklyn-born, fruitarian, cloak-and-suiter background into the very model of overachieverdom. She runs three businesses. She personally convinced the California small business administration out of a $1.67-million loan to finance the building of the new Door. In a masterstroke of financial wizardry, she qualified for that loan by separating her businesses into separate corporations so the Door—with its annual gross of a million-plus dollars a year—might still be considered small. The income generated by the more Spartan retreat in Tecate—with its payroll-cutting device of American "apprentices" working for room and board—never came under examination. (Once these employees cross the border into California, their salaries are the factor which, in Mazzanti's view, keeps the Golden Door payroll and guest fee so high: "With the services industry, almost half the Door's gross goes to payroll.")

It's doubtful that Deborah Szainman Szekely, the eighteen-year-old bride of naturalist Edmond Bordeaux Szekely, ever dreamed she'd have to worry about $497,-000 payrolls. And certainly she and the Professor (as she called him) weren't thinking about the minimum-wage advantages when they opened their farm in Mexico in 1940. The Door's grandparent was a working ranch: Guests lived in tents and paid the Szekelys $17.50 a week for the privilege of being able to work there, plow the fields, and make goat cheese. "In those days, the Professor and I did everything," Mazzanti remembers. "It was fun. I've always had lots of energy, so I enjoyed it."

Deborah Szainman was more than ready to take on a bizarre marriage; her mother was a strict fruitarian, a 1925 vice-president of the New York City Vegetarian Society. Her father's cloak-and-suit business was thriving. "When the Depression came along," Mazzanti says, "we couldn't get all our fruit, and Daddy had lost all his money, but not quite. Mother said he was feeling very despondent, and all his friends were doing away with themselves. He was really very blue. She said it was just a question of thinking, 'Let's change and go where there's fresh fruit.' That's when we went to Tahiti." The Szainmans stayed there four and a half years. "It was only when he made so much money [exporting coconut oil] that he had to come back to America and prove he wasn't a failure."

From the exile of Tahiti, Deborah returned to a different kind of exile. In San Francisco she felt "like an outsider" as a teenager; by eighteen, her parents were happy to endorse her marriage to the vegetarian-philosopher she'd met when he came to visit her parents on Tahiti. Later, she'd pick up a second husband—Vincent Mazzanti, a La Jolla psychoanalyst—as well as a turn-of-the-century hillside home and an income estimated at $200,000 a year. Along the way, she kept the best of her Zentellectual training while mastering the intricacies of corporate finance. It's that duality which inspires her guests, not her dietary regime. Mazzanti is simply a living tribute to overachievement. "When you read a *Who's Who* profile that's two inches long and one that's two paragraphs, the one who did more obviously had more energy and a better time in life," she preaches.

Her guests reflect her orientation; over a third of them now are businesswomen. Their median age has dropped from the forty-pluses who sign on for Maine Chance to the more vital mid-thirties woman who is more inclined to thrive on an Outward Bound for the Radically Chic with only a touch of Narcissist's Heaven. In addition to men's weeks, there are now couples' weeks, budget weeks (Thanksgiving, Easter, and Christmas), and Menninger Foundation weeks. During the spring and summer, the Door is booked months in advance; at no time, apparently, does anyone balk at the price. "That doesn't worry them at all," Mazzanti explains. "We originally started at two hundred and fifty dollars a week. That was as much as twelve hundred and fifty dollars is now. Think about all those thousand-dollar dresses that Saks, Bonwit, and Bergdorf carry—you'd be shocked at the number they sell. The dress lasts only so long. It has nothing to do with the body underneath."

Her clients may not dispute her claim that $250 in 1960 equals $1,250 in 1970, but the inflationary experts do; that $250 is now about $450, they say. When pressed on this point, Mazzanti refers to that $1.67-million loan that needs repayment. She is never challenged further. The Golden Door, after all, is a refuge from that bottom-line worldliness. Talk shifts to more intimately worldly matters. Antoinette Hatfield wants a title for her new cookbook, her third. Liz Carpenter organizes a cocktail-hour contest. The Dallas art dealer and Mrs. Stocking Fortune collide. "Where did you get that watch?" the Stocking Fortune wonders. "Cartier's. Where'd you get yours?" "Cartier's . . . *Paris,*" the stocking fortune retorts.

With pounds holding as steady as *Happy Days'* ratings, dinner-table conversations begin to verge on the unladylike. The Lockheed worker tries to convince Mrs. Starkist about the wisdom of psychic healing, then gets miffed when she wins no response. "You haven't heard of Jack Schwartz? He's world-famous!" On Friday night, the single waitress is slow bringing out the veal scaloppine *champignon.* "I can't believe this!" the Textile Mill screams. "We've been waiting for twenty-five minutes and there's still no dinner. Those entrees should be on our place mats the very minute the salads are whisked away."

There are interludes. Yuchi, a Korean dancer from Los Angeles who's a *Sonny and Cher* regular, is flown down to give the Friday class. He teaches the North Carolina Republican to get up and boogie; for a few minutes, libido crackles. "Look at the way my stomach's sticking out!" the House of Jewels yells. The Korean remains admirably sphinxlike as fantasies are shattered throughout the room.

At five o'clock, yoga is being taught. "Inhale vitality, exhale disease. Inhale tranquility, exhale stress." The Lockheed worker forgets this as soon as Deborah appears for her ritual Saturday-night lecture. After a long hour of obviously stale material about "the importance of the psychological calorie" and the virtues of jumping into an exercise suit before you reach for the coffee, Mazzanti is unceremoniously interrupted. "Do you follow all those things you say?" the shift worker demands. Mazzanti explains that she's too busy running a company that employs two hundred people to worry about little things like routinized calisthenics—or the two glasses of

Marie Brenner

champagne she downed along with the evening's festive dinner. "So what? A lot of us work," the Lockheed worker continues. "Why should we follow these teachings when you obviously don't? Or you wouldn't look the way you do!"

It is, as they say, a tense moment. The women breathe very quietly. Not because this is the crucial question, the zinger that could tip group opinion against the Door. The question is: How will Deborah handle this witch? Bad enough that Miss Lockheed should scream at the scheduling girl that morning, "All of these women are rich snobs! Nobody waits for me for lunch or dinner!" Worse that she should attack Deborah. These women understand that Deborah's no paragon, that she's running a business that's already successful and wants it to be more so. In the silence that follows, Mazzanti lets Lockheed's tirade evaporate, like a pound that shouldn't have been there in the first place.

But that self-righteous anger points up what may be the Door's biggest problem: how to respond to media-drenched harpies who, when est and the nip-and-tuck haven't worked, come to the Door to be reborn. Because the Golden Door neither promises or delivers any miracles. Its guests are simply given an opportunity to eat a total of 4,900 calories for an entire week and burn off perhaps three times that many in an atmosphere that is less depressing than Maine Chance or the Green House. "A mental douche," one woman dubbed it. A chance to escape the collective pressures of jobs and families and look briefly through the keyhole into life as it's enjoyed by the very upper middle class. Nothing more, nothing less. Take away what you can, apply it if you will, but by all means, while you're at the Door, go with its flow.

Do not, then, expect to find the ideal affair waiting at

the Door; there is very little sex since the old Michel left. There is, in fact, very little in the way of high jinks. In April, three women broke into the kitchen and put some bread and honey in front of another guest's door. A guest who bragged she was Helena Rubinstein's granddaughter sneaked her boyfriend in for a night-long visit. A spy from Vic Tanny's titillated some housewives around the pool with made-up adventures of her life as a pornographer.

But these moments are as rare as Escondido rain. The Door hums along almost all of the time, a quietly efficient factory where the machinery is, if not invisible, at least swathed in velvet. "I can't wait to get out of here," the Dallas art dealer groused on her last day. But would she return? "Absolutely." So would at least twenty of her spa-mates. For all the shakeups in the staff, the gripes with the business-first ethic of the management, and the pamper-me attitudes of some of the less-worldly guests, those who have graduated from a week at the Golden Door consider themselves among the elect. It may cost them about half as much as a Toyota, but for the chance to be deeply shallow, as Mazzanti well understands, any price is a bargain.

ON THE
WAY DOWN

THE TRIALS
OF TOM LAUGHLIN

"**B**ILLY!" screams an eight-months-pregnant teenager at Hollywood's St. Anne's Maternity Hospital. "Do you have any Indian in you?" It's not *Billy*, it's *Tom*, Tom Laughlin, the 44-year-old producer-director-star of *Billy Jack* and *The Trial of Billy Jack*. But to the 40 million Americans who have seen him aikido-kick his way through corruption in these movies (which have grossed more than $60 million), he and his holy half-breed screen persona are one and the same. His fans do not know that Tom Laughlin is the Huey Long of the film industry, a 220-pound ex-football player turned film tycoon given to violent rages. They do not know about the lawsuits. They do not know about the ultrasophisticated alarm systems guarding his Brentwood house, the Jungian dream analysis, the threats, the ranting, the vendettas. They certainly do not know that Laughlin is currently constructing a media campaign to make Billy Jack a populist political savior. The unwed mothers, along with the rest of Laughlin's constituency, think of him simply as incorruptible Billy Jack. Which suits Laughlin fine. For now.

"Do I have any Indian in me?" he repeats in the most absolute of monotones. "No." They sigh as a group.

"Well, we really do have a medicine man who took me

through that," Laughlin amends. "I apologized to him for not being a true Indian, and he said, 'Being an Indian is not just a matter of birth.' He said I was the first *spiritual* Indian ever to appear in films." Laughlin shifts his bulk, uncomfortable in his dress-up clothes: chartreuse-and-black ski jacket, black pants, loafers. The questions are routine enough, but he is hungry—he nibbles at chocolate chips during the questions—and starting to get angry. The pale yellow "target memo," one of dozens processed by his three secretaries and one assistant each day, has clearly stated there would be dinner. And here he is in a cafeteria, looking for the buffet table, sandwiches, any parody of a meal, and all he sees are the beaming faces of 83 pregnant admirers.

"Billy!" shouts a Katharine Ross look-alike. "Where's T.C. tonight?"

"Our daughter wasn't feeling well," Laughlin lies. "My wife, Dody [actress Delores Taylor], is home taking care of her."

Billy-Billy-Billy-Billy-Billy!! A dozen hands are in the air reaching for Laughlin's attention. A girl in the front wins. Her eyes are wide; she stumbles over her words, twirling the peppermint carnation that each girl has been given on this special night. "Is everything in the movie really true?"

"What's really important about a movie like *Billy Jack,* " Laughlin answers, "is the healing effect it can have on people—like you and me—and their lives." The teenagers squeal for recognition, waving their flowers, unaware that Billy is launching into a set piece. His face clouds, the furrows forming a veritable relief map of the Rio Grande. "Wonder if I could have your attention for a moment." Incredibly, they ignore him. Louder, his smile frozen, his mouth tight, he tries to get them back in control. *"Wonder if I could have your attention!"* As they hush, the afterimage of anger disappears; once again he is their charming Billy.

"Every day I get letters. Thousands of letters. One day I got a letter from a girl in North Carolina. 'Dear Mr. Laughlin,' she said, 'I am my mother's sole support. I can't believe it, I am shocked by what is going on around me. The woman who owns my nursery school is serving jelly sandwiches and water to the kids and pocketing the government subsidy, the funds the government sends her for the lunches. What should I do?' . . ."

He drones on, and suddenly it is three weeks earlier, an April afternoon, and Laughlin, in red-white-and-blue sneakers and jogging suit, is telling the same story in precisely the same words at Billy Jack headquarters, David O. Selznick's old offices in Culver City. ". . . I wrote her back. I hated to do it. I said, 'There is nothing you can do. *Yet.* Your mother needs you more. Wait.' But that's not the end. I got another letter, same girl. 'I couldn't wait any longer, I had to do something. I called the federal inspectors and had them come see for themselves.' Do you know what? The woman who owned the nursery bought them off. And the girl got fired."

"Oh no," voices murmured around the office, a counterpoint to the crackling of the fire—just as the girls at St. Anne's murmur and gasp at the fate of the girl who could have been any one of them. If only she had listened to Billy Jack!

If only everyone would listen. "We were scouting for *Billy Jack* locations," Laughlin remembers, pacing in his Brentwood compound. "We were somewhere up north at a tiny airport. It was me, the crew, and the Indian medicine man I always travel with. Suddenly, just as we're getting ready to get on this little Piper cub, a huge owl landed on the bright neon Shell sign at the edge of the runway. Well, if you know anything about owls, you know that they just don't do that. The crew got very scared, because the Navahos consider the owl a messenger of death. None of them would get on that plane. I asked the medicine man what the owl meant, so he went over to a dark place, laid out all his things, and smoked. I sat behind him, waiting—remember, this was 1969; we'd just gotten the money for *Billy Jack;* we were ecstatic. Finally, the medicine man spoke: 'Tom, this is not a symbol of death. But the owl has a very heavy message for you. The film you are about to shoot will have a greater impact on American youth than any film ever made.' "

Laughlin pauses, rocking below the bookshelf with its seven remaindered copies of Jung's *Man and His Symbols.* "The medicine man went on: 'You are going to have to prepare yourself for three years of the most unmitigated obstacles—sheer hell—you have ever been through, but at the end of those three years, it will be okay.' And," says Laughlin, forcing some inflection in his voice, "it *was* at the end of those three years—almost to the day—that we settled our lawsuit with Warner Brothers, and it was in May that our four-walling campaign took off; but *during* those years we had to endure shutting down our company, almost going bankrupt, then the AIP suit, then the fight with Fox, finally winding up at Warner's, then the problem there till the settlement. And I thought the Indian was crazy. . . ."

Unfortunately, the Indian and the owl weren't around last spring when Billy Jack declared war on the critics. Which happened because Laughlin, having released *The Trial of Billy Jack* in November, decided that $25 million worth of business in the first five weeks wasn't enough. He pulled the picture from the theaters after Christmas, assuming that when he brought *Trial* back to Billy Jack's fans in the spring, they'd be lined up around the block. He'd have to launch another massive ad campaign anyway; why not tie it to one of his causes?

The Critics Contest began with full-page ads in newspapers from the *San Diego Union* to *The New York Times.* Warner Brothers advanced Laughlin the $600,000 for prizes, theater bookings, and ads that pitted "Billy Jack vs. the Critics" over a head (and seventeen-inch neck) shot of Laughlin in his cigar-store-Indian Stetson. The ad copy was a 5,000-word "open letter" from Laughlin, an agate-type paean to *Billy Jack*'s greatness, with supporting quotes from *Cahiers du Cinéma.* You didn't even have to write the 300-word essay ("Why are the critics so out of touch with audiences?") to win the sweepstakes.

No one in the Laughlin offices during those last giddy weeks in April anticipated that the contest would be a total disaster. "I just got off the phone with David Begelman [president of Columbia Pictures, former head of Creative Management Associates]," Laughlin gloated one afternoon. "Begelman said to me, 'Tom, you're doing the very same thing I've always wanted to do. I admire you. It's about time someone took on the critics.' " Three staff members sitting on the couch nodded. "But what I didn't tell Begelman," Laughlin concluded triumphantly, "was that the *next* group I'm taking on are ex-agents who run studios."

First, though, he'd have to slaughter those critics— single-handedly. Because not only had just a niggling "few thousand" essays dribbled in, but the rerelease of *Trial,* too soon after its original opening, was equally disastrous. Still, Laughlin would not concede defeat: "I'm going to write a paperback book," he said with his customary zeal, "taking on each critic, pulling out his reviews, proving the dichotomy between each critic and the preferences of the popular audience."

Marie Brenner

But Vincent Canby, Pauline Kael, Judith Crist—they are only minor Laughlin targets. His enemies list includes: conglomerates, the National Rifle Association, the nuclear power industry, Indian-haters, the TV networks, big business in general, Rockefeller in particular, the FTC, the oil cartel, Nixon and "the Ehrlichman mentality," cigarettes, alcohol, soda pop, and "the spineless, weak moguls who are running the film studios." And this Waldorf salad of hates is only openers, targets of the Good Tom.

Even his friends admit there are two Laughlins—one the crusading idealist, the other spiteful and violent, convinced that people are out to get or "betray" him. Others maintain that there are indeed two Laughlins, but they are more like the Bad Tom and the Worse Tom.

The Laughlin split personality resembles the split in Billy Jack's screen personality. Billy—for the 170 million Americans who haven't bought tickets— is a peace-loving Indian who preaches love and leftist ideals, helping a progressive schoolmarm, played by his wife, Delores ("Dody") Taylor, run her interrracial Freedom School. Billy Jack is sanguine, until he gets crossed. Then, the pacific Indian turns into a karate monster, a killer for peace.

Like Billy when he's on the warpath, Bad Tom flies into chemical rages, only Laughlin's are slightly less lethal. No aikido (except for the chops he gives to the walls), but his face turns florid, his voice breaks a thousand decibels as he yells at a secretary: *"Who do you think you are? You have destroyed my creative processes by walking into this meeting. If I were Paul Newman, I'd throw you off the set. If I were Clint Eastwood, I would have your ass kicked off this picture."* The truly possessed Laughlin makes exactly the same speech, but for emphasis picks up a clock radio and hurls it at the offending secretary.

A close family friend remembers having to drive Dody to the hospital after a family argument. Tom himself told a group of high-school kids in June, 1974: "I beat the shit out of my wife for many years, I'm one of those. . . . What I had to do was try to come to a point where I could stop beating my wife." (He apparently succeeded via Jungian dream therapy.)

Tom's temper has landed him in court. There is still an assault charge pending against him dating back two and a half years, when he gave a director named Jack Spear a bloody lip for delivering a commercial a day late. But many of the 24 lawsuits filed against Laughlin since 1970 are over money he allegedly owes the plaintiffs. "You just can't keep making your own laws," Dody tells the hero of *Billy Jack.* "Fine," Billy replies, "and when that set of laws is fairly applied to everyone, then I'll turn the other cheek, too." In real life, Laughlin does not turn the other cheek. He spends $500,000 a year on legal fees because, he explains, suing Billy Jack "is an 'in' game, and people think it will get them a lot of attention. They think we'll give them $15,000 to settle. All the lawsuits are that crazy. . . ."

It's not easy for Tom Laughlin to talk about his early years. "I have never understood why someone would find someone's childhood—all that psychohistory—interesting," he says. Finally, he relents: "We were poor. On welfare a lot. I thought it was incredibly magical that other families had cars. . . ."

Laughlin is not close to his family. He told a group of high-school kids, "My mother was really screwed up, my father was, too. She was a bitch. He was a nice guy. They left me with enormous scars. At fourteen, I was in pain all the time." It's not surprising that today Laughlin is obsessed by what Jung calls the *anima*—the female within—and rarely dispenses more affection than a playful headlock. Never in *Billy Jack* do he and Dody kiss.

Always, he was a fighter. He describes his school days as a series of hard-fought victories, *me against them.* How he defended the only black kid in the third grade against a racist teacher. How "by just talking to the guys, *reasoning with them,* " a sixteen-year-old Tom was able to cool down the bullies who were angry that he was making time with the rich girls in their high school.

"I was always the wild kid, the troublemaker, but still the leader," Laughlin says. It didn't stop when he got to the University of Wisconsin, where he played football and was so good that "men would leave cash in envelopes at the clothing stores for me; it used to really bother me—these were decent men." (But he took the envelopes.) He describes himself as a "tramp athlete," going from Wisconsin to Marquette playing ball, landing on probation, and meeting Dody, who had grown up near a South Dakota Indian reservation. They married and—young, attractive, and broke—talked about making it in the movies. Eventually, with Dody seven months pregnant, they headed for Hollywood, where they hung around the Pasadena Playhouse, living on "milk, pork, macaroni, and beans" while they waited to be discovered. That was in 1955. Before the plywood wall.

Thank God for that plywood wall. Without it there might never have been a *Billy Jack.* It happened this way: Laughlin and Dody were still hanging around the Pasadena Playhouse, dirt poor, now further encumbered by their two-year-old son, Frank. By chance, director William Wellman spotted Tom's Smithfield-ham arms and cast him in *Lafayette Escadrille.* On the set, a stunt man dove through a paper wall and muffed the take. There was no other fake wall ready to go, and Wellman was furious. Then, *deus ex machina* in the form of Tom Laughlin, who volunteered his 200 pounds of football muscle to break through a real plywood wall. Wellman agreed. The cameras rolled. Laughlin smashed through an inch and a half of plywood, a perfect take. Wellman said, "You're my kind of man, son," and the aging director took the young actor under his wing and helped him get parts.

The Laughlins struggled on. Tom got bit parts but wasn't really going anywhere. Both he and Dody had become fiercely ambitious, determined to make their own films. Every extra penny they made went into renting film equipment ("We'd cheat and rent it on a Saturday, so we could get an extra free day"). It took them three years, but they made *The Proper Time* ("When it looked like we might have to scrap the whole thing, a friend mortgaged his house, gave us $15,000. I vowed that when I got successful, I would do that same kind of thing for others"). United Artists released the film, but it never took off, although UA called Laughlin "a young Orson Welles" and offered him a contract. But, after ten weeks, Laughlin bridled under the authority and left.

He turned instead to running a school. The Laughlins' son, Frank, was five, and their second child, Teresa Christina ("T.C."), was two. Dody and Tom heard about the Montessori method, and with the money they received for *The Proper Time,* they opened the Sophia Montessori School in their house.

And then the problems began. Laughlin had told the parents of the early joiners that his school was nonprofit, so over the summer of 1960 they all pitched in, donating time and services. But only months after the Sophia Montessori School was underway, the Brentwood parents were at odds with Laughlin. They accused him of ripping the school off, claiming that though he had promised the school would be nonprofit, he was charging

$1,000 a student and had not applied for nonprofit status from the IRS. Laughlin said he was flying to Chicago where "an investment house" would put up $500,000 for "a chain" of Montessori schools, but a parent who called to check out this investment house found no listing for it in all of Illinois. The loan did not materialize.

The Brentwood fathers had confronted Laughlin, offering to buy him out. Laughlin countered: "It's my school, I can run it any way I want to." He would, he said, refuse to readmit a student if the father did not desist from complaining. "I will not allow you to molest my child that way!" the father yelled. A few weeks later, at another parents' meeting, a weary Laughlin: "To show you how vicious, how distorted, the lengths some parents will go to, I have even been accused of child-molesting."

During this period, Laughlin took to recording his dreams, to "devoting time to the psyche." And in his spare time he made another film, *We Are All Christ,* an allegory in which he played a Jesus figure. United Screen Arts picked it up, changed its title to *The Young Sinner,* and released it into oblivion. Meantime, the 1965 school catalog was an opulent extravaganza, all ecru bonded paper and soft-focus photography, dreamy with promises that the "expansion program" of 1965 would extend the Sophia Montessori School into "one of the most exciting four-year liberal-arts colleges in the country." Instead, he and it went bankrupt. While parents blamed mismanagement, Laughlin blamed overexpansion.

There was no end to Laughlin's woes. His furniture was repossessed. ("People would spit on us, literally.") His children had to sleep on the floor. In May of 1965, an English secretarial applicant was strangled at Tom's Montessori school, and her body was found in a nearby garage. Laughlin was questioned before police finally arrested a 23-year-old janitor, who later confessed. Meantime, Laughlin was living off advances, scrounging loans.

Then, on an airplane, he met a stewardess named Elizabeth James. He said she had a "great look," and promised her the starring role in his next movie—but she'd have to write it. Incredibly, she did—on speculation—and the result was the 1967 feature *Born Losers,* financed by backers in Oklahoma looking for a movie tax shelter. It was this motorcycle-cult film that introduced half-breed ex-Green Beret Billy Jack to the world. "Dody and I wrote this picture, of course," Laughlin says today. But the screen credit reads "James Lloyd," Elizabeth James's pseudonym, and the Writers Guild credited "E. James Lloyd."

Toward the end of shooting on *Born Losers,* Laughlin came down with appendicitis and had to have his stomach packed with ice each night so he wouldn't have to give his enemies the satisfaction of seeing him shut down production. Finally, Sam Arkoff of American International Pictures distributed the film.

And then came *Billy Jack,* which Twentieth Century–Fox agreed to release. Laughlin worked on it with Elizabeth James for a year; then he fired her, without pay, giving her role to an older, blonder actress—wife Dody.

Billy Jack was finished in 1971. But Laughlin tells a story about Dick Zanuck, of Fox, who was a Republican delegate at the 1972 convention, demanding changes, sending a memo: "We cannot release this movie. Without a lot of cuts, it would be too political." (Zanuck denies ever having sent such a memo.) The mythology continues. Laughlin brags that Zanuck had gone over to the storage vault to steal the print and edit it himself. "I wasn't going to stand for that," Laughlin said. "I ran out to the sound lab, found he hadn't gotten there yet, and stole my own master tapes—you can't release a picture without a sound track, can you? I buried them under my bed. There was no way Fox was going to get at the sound track without first plowing through me."

Finally, Fox sold Laughlin back his film for $100,000, and the search was on for a new distributor. It wasn't easy. A Bel-Air producer told Laughlin, "This movie will never make a dime." But when Ted Ashley, then chairman of Warner Brothers, screened a print at home one night and his wife cried, the *Billy Jack* industry was off and running. More or less.

Tom Laughlin was still fighting. One battle was with his landlord, over some $50,000 back rent he owed on his twenty-fourth-floor offices in Century City. When the landlord started to hassle him, Laughlin yelled, "Why don't you meet me out in the hall?" Fortunately, the landlord had an alternative—a Laughlin associate, Charlie Kettering, Jr., was the lease's guarantor. Unfortunately, however, Kettering ran out on a Denver street to save his dog from being run over and was run over himself. (Eventually the Kettering estate had to make good the debt, which Laughlin got around to repaying over the next few years.)

The really big battle was to be with Warner's after *Billy Jack* was released and had begun to sink. "Someday you are going to realize that I am Stanley Kubrick and John Wayne combined," Laughlin told a producer, but Warner's didn't see it. Leo Greenfield, head of sales, let it be known that he thought the picture was garbage, and he socked it into drive-ins, porno houses, the B-pic graveyard. Outraged, Laughlin sued Warner Brothers for $34 million, charging mishandling. What Laughlin got was the right to distribute his movie in New York, Chicago, and Los Angeles.

Enter four-walling, a 1930s distribution idea which

was revived successfully in the sixties by the makers of low-budget nature films. All the distributor had to do was rent a theater for a set fee and then keep all the receipts—or suffer all the losses. Laughlin rented dozens of theaters to cover each city's neighborhoods, then blitzed the local airways with TV spots. And the results made movie history: *Billy Jack* (a rerelease, yet!) set records everywhere and earned over $20 million, of which Laughlin had 48 percent. (He has since turned down TV offers of $4 million for the film, figuring his theater audience will be out there for yet another sweep.)

He didn't waste any time starting on a sequel to *Billy Jack,* which he would finance and distribute himself. The budget was set at $2.5 million, and when *The Trial of Billy Jack* was released in November, 1974, Laughlin had sunk $7.5 million in a massive thousand-theater distribution pattern (four-walled only in a few major cities) and a high-saturation TV campaign. He also demanded—and got—$8,000 to $10,000 in cash advances from each theater, assuring him, before a single showing of his film, that each customer dollar would be clear profit.

Good Tom could afford to become a philanthropist. But when his newly formed Billy Jack Foundation gave $20,000 to an Indian couple who wanted to start a magazine about Indian affairs, they disappeared with the money. He started another Montessori school in his house—on weekends—and when the Brentwood Neighbors Association complained that the school was in violation of the local zoning ordinances, Laughlin ignored them.

In 1974 an expansive Laughlin opened a record company and a separate distribution company, filling his offices on the dilapidated old Selznick lot with a staff of 100. Former employees—Laughlin has one of the highest turnover rates in Hollywood—remember how much of his energy went into memos. Everywhere he went, he carried his Sony: "This is Tom Laughlin. I have a verbal going to Frank Wells, Warner Brothers." The tapes got transcribed by his three secretaries, who filed red copies under memos and green ones in the Dream Files. Everything was color-coded, checked, double-checked. Nothing was too trivial for attention. One memo directed Billy Jack employees not to speak to the boss on his way in or out of the john ("Tom doesn't want his creative processes disturbed"). That memo was signed by Dody, but it was pure Tom. He again used Dody's name on the infamous Billy's-getting-fat memo (now selling for 25 cents a copy in Paris), which blamed the staff for "interfacing" with the creative genius too frequently, causing his avoirdupois. "We are killing the goose that is laying all our golden eggs," it read.

He ended up creating a quasi-military operation. And appropriately, he hired ex-Under Secretary of Defense and former Litton Industries military specialist John Rubel as his chief financial officer. Rubel makes $120,-000 a year at Billy Jack, upgrading the television advertising strategy, breaking the country down in a city-by-city analysis. Every few weeks, when Laughlin discovers a flaw in the system, he goes berserk. Another meeting is called, more employees are hired, more procedures instituted.

Billy Jack's Brentwood home, which used to belong to Cloris Leachman, is full of systems too. An entertainment system includes a screening room, recording studio, gym, pool room, tennis courts, and ice-cream bar. "The day I buy a Rolls-Royce is the day I know something will have gone dead in me," Laughlin says. Instead, he has invested $100,000 in an electronic security wall so sophisticated that he bragged to Motown Industries chairman Berry Gordy, "Even an ex-CIA guy and an ex-FBI guy I hired couldn't get past it."

Inside, there are signs everywhere. One reads, "We Thank You for Not Smoking," and if you ignore it, the alarm system is triggered. When actor James Franciscus lit his pipe, the Fire Department was at the door in minutes. Paramount chairman Barry Diller makes sure he's well outside the house before pulling out a Winston.

Laughlin's home is his barricade. His chauffeur is a karate master. Secretaries must park two blocks away so their cars do not clutter the vista. The press is not welcome. "What do you mean I have to give interviews!" Laughlin screamed at a PR man. "Nixon gets written about all the time and *he* doesn't give interviews."

Billy Jack is not a screen character; he is a way of life. Tom Laughlin has hired a new president, John Burke, to run his company so he can devote his energies to filmmaking. Or perhaps teaching. Or perhaps the magazine he is planning to publish. ("It will be one-third investigative pieces, one-third pieces on the arts, and one-third how-to guide, to really show people through litigation, through all kinds of means, how they can start making their government more accountable. Sy Hersh, Bernstein, and Woodward are the best investigative reporters? I'll hire them.")

There might even be time to brood about the failure of *The Trial* on its second run. Always he'll have the nagging doubt that his movies have succeeded more because of their mass-market ad campaigns than because of any deep public identification with the Billy Jack messiah. "Jesus," Laughlin sighed one month after *The Trial* flopped, "I hope people aren't beginning to think that just because a movie is advertised a lot on TV, it's junk."

Meantime, he's working on the fall release of a movie called *The Master Gunfighter,* in which he plays a nineteenth-century Billy. And on *The Deadliest Spy,* about industrial espionage. And, working with Jane Fonda on a film about Karen Silkwood, the young woman who died trying to expose conditions in an Oklahoma plutonium plant. And, of course, he's deep into *Billy Jack III*—which he claims Ralph Nader will be working on as a consultant —and which, he explains, "will provide a blueprint showing how to organize your neighborhood, because no political change can be wrought in the United States until there is a revolution at the local level."

Billy Jack is not kidding. Most people who meet Laughlin are genuinely terrified of him. (Composer Elmer Bernstein said before his first scoring session on *The Trial of Billy Jack,* "You are looking at one scared Jew.") Tom Laughlin has plans. "I have a vision that Billy Jack will institute great political changes," he intones.

Nonsense? Ask George McGovern. He took Billy Jack along on a train trip through Nebraska. The candidate's staff thought Laughlin was strictly Kiwanis Club. Then they pulled into a small town, and McGovern brought out Tom and Dody almost as an afterthought—his star campaigners, Warren Beatty and Shirley MacLaine, were elsewhere—and the crowd went wild. The local high-school band—impromptu— struck up "One Tin Soldier," the theme from *Billy Jack,* and the people began to sing, solemnly, in unison:

"Go ahead and hate your neighbor/Go ahead and cheat a friend/ . . . On the bloody morning after one tin soldier rides away. . . ."

THE GOSPEL ACCORDING TO BILLY JACK

On intellectuals: "The intellectual hates emotions and is frightened by them, so he hides behind ideas. . . . Never trust a man with ideas."

Going Hollywood

On fighting corruption: "Watergate was nothing more than a melodrama about honest people fighting gangsters, corruption. I'm doing the same thing in *Billy Jack*—just on a different level—and a lot of people are rooting for me to win. *Billy Jack* is more than a movie. It makes the individual feel like he can go out and do something about corruption. *Billy Jack* is a philosophy of life."

On simplifying life: "Life is too complicated in this country. Recently, in Washington, Ralph Nader handed me a report that was three inches thick on what simple citizens can do—you and me—to control the spread of nuclear industries. When Nader handed me this, I said, 'I can't read this. Give it to me in six concise sheets or I don't want to know it.' "

On becoming President: "I'd be the worst President in the world. I polarize people. When I see something, I want to fix it right away, I don't want any deliberations. If I were the President, I would have Washington so divided—paralyzed . . . that I mean even John Kennedy had it polarized and he was able to be much more of a politician than I would be."

On intelligence: "I had the highest I.Q. of anyone who was in the Milwaukee school system [with me] at the time . . . I know I've ranged as low as 149–52 and I think—they used to test me all the time, it was a phenomenon—it went as high as 180, maybe 190."

On idols: "The youth of this country have only two heroes: Ralph Nader and Billy Jack."

NELSON

FINAL TRIBUTE: *CHER*

On the face of it she was as smarmy and as silly as one of her routines. She was the ultimate parody —Lily Tomlin playing Cher—but somehow when the clapping stopped, only the little Indian with the hair to her waist and the bugle beads and the electric navel was left—she couldn't step out of her role. From the Girl Scout of acid rock, she had grown up into Barbi Benton. She was a sex symbol, but she had no breasts. Just layer after layer of those sequins and the individually glued Perma-lashes and the Daniel Eastman pancake for the hot lights. She said that was why her skin broke out, the pancake make-up under the hot lights.

Except she always had zits, even when she was a kid, a scrawny teenager cruising Sunset, checking out the fan mags at the Safeway, wearing cashmeres, talking on her Princess phone, skipping classes at Montclair Prep, singing in the back of the art room with 31 flavors' Edie Baskin, walking down the halls with little Sinatras or baby Ray Charles. She was a Los Angeles child, a daughter of the Golden Dream. By age sixteen, she had dropped out and run away from home. Her mother was on husband number five. The year was 1962.

By 1964, she was Mrs. Sonny Bono, and she had begun to sing. His songs, like "I Got You, Babe," created her;

she wallowed in it and she let us do her in. Not a cliché would pass her by, not a turn of popular phrase, not a fad or a gesture; she never missed the slightest nuance of what was in or what was hot. She could be a Streisand or a Midler; perhaps if she'd met Charlie Manson instead of Sonny Bono, she might have wound up a Squeaky Fromme. She was a sponge, a sieve, a mirror of the times, only nobody was letting her in on the joke. Not CBS, not Sonny, not her mother (now on husband number eight), not her analyst, not her est trainer, not her beauty min-yan. Even those who owned a piece of her contributed to her fall: Her press agent cranked out material on her pregnancies and abortion, her talent agent hyped her as perfect to play a car thief. Everything backfired: Ex-husbands sued boyfriends, her second marriage was over almost before it began, she glommed from man to man, and in the midst of it her father filed suit against her, charging Cher with invasion of his privacy and damage to his "business relationships." Around the same time, she saved the Average White Band's lead singer's life.

In 1975, there was a new-model Cher, the woman alone. She would make it in a man's world, by herself; she would tough it out. She was, everybody knew, just a street kid. Even if she wore five-thousand-dollar dresses, even if she lived in thirty-two rooms. What she didn't count on was that nobody could imagine Pat Loud without Bill; nobody wanted Erin Fleming without Groucho Marx. Cher alone didn't have a chance.

She was over, but she took a year to crash. First came the hype, the 747 of a media campaign to prove she could make it in the world alone. Tragic how they pumped her into grotesquerie, poured her into two tons of Moll Flanders costumes and outsize wigs, Bob Mackie soufflé nets. They made her kabuki theater and tried to clean her up. For comedy, she hurled bricks at refrigerators or pretended she couldn't snag a man. They debased her, made her a walking joke. Each week she'd bring home $25,000, but the handwriting was on the wall.

And clearly on the financial page. The hot stock was to have been Megoin, Inc., on the Amex. They guaranteed thousands of Cher dolls would flood the stores by Christmas; what was at 12 could go to 20, maybe even double. That's what the Beverly Hills brokers were saying in October. By December it had bounced to 10, then dribbled down to 9. CBS had thrown her up against the *Six Million Dollar Man,* and Cher—the woman alone—didn't have the stuff. She bombed. Her ratings slipped.

Still, they wouldn't let her go with grace, wouldn't quietly pull the plug or put her out to pasture. SONNY AND CHER MAKE IT OFFICIAL, *Variety* screamed. THEY'LL TEAM AGAIN (BIZ ONLY) . Their new venture begins on February 1, at eight, on CBS. Though her fans have seen her falter, her failure has been papered over, as if she had never stumbled. So quickly was the classic duo recycled, perhaps they hope we'll forget we saw her fall.

But we can't and we won't. The dog reminds us of the pony, and without each other there is no act. Standing next to Sonny at their Beverly Hills press conference, Cher was oddly quiet, an unwilling lovebird returned to her mate's gilded cage. Sonny was jubilant, but then, he was never immortalized on the cover of *Time.* He was not one of *People*'s "most intriguing" people of 1975. But Cher was—and Cher isn't. Neither lovebird is a star— only, at most, half a star. At the press conference there was scattered applause, but it was hollow, like the sound of one hand clapping.

WHATEVER HAPPENED TO ALI MACGRAW?

She was the golden girl, an Ivy League Miss America, a romantic ideal mythologized on the cover of *Time*. She appeared like a daffodil, tolling the death knell to the sixties, signifying a return to all that was wholesome. Her blue jeans were clean, her long dark hair was sleek and shining, her crooked teeth made her more than just another beauty. She was the girl next door, everyone's fantasy.

She had been brought up on it. Her parents were artists, seeped in the world of Rackin and Dulac. As a child in Pound Ridge, New York, she spent hours drawing perfect little pictures, illustrating her poems, weaving dreams for herself. Children's dreams starring Prince Charming, perhaps. Dreams that her dolls played out in the special house her mother had built for her one Christmas. The wallpaper was perfect, hand-tinted; there was even a miniature chandelier. Her penmanship was the best in the class. Her grades were high. But she kept her illusions, the remnants of fairy tales she had played out even as a very little girl with long, flowing dark hair.

Everywhere you go, people wonder what happened to the golden girl. They're especially curious at Ron Fletcher's, where Beverly Hills' other golden girls elongate their thighs. Cher, for example, might turn to Candy Bergen and say, "Why doesn't Ali come around any more?"

Because Ali MacGraw never used to miss a day. It had been part of her ritual even when she lived an hour away. Up early, the sun coming over the Malibu mountains, shining into the glass house she shares with husband Steve McQueen. A simple house, filled with plants, a few prints. Nothing grand. A secret house—McQueen shrouded her like a precious flower; the mail went to a Gulf Station down the Pacific Coast Highway.

Joshua, her son, was six, looking more and more like his father, Paramount producer Bob Evans. Daily she would bundle him up, hurry him into the brown Mercedes convertible, hustle him off to school. Then she would zoom south; with good traffic she could be at Ron Fletcher's by ten, maybe a hair sooner. And there she'd stay. Black leotards chopped off at the ankles, her long bony feet (her worst feature) clutched to the steel bar in a prehensile position while the springs would dig into her shoulders, and then, very carefully, her pelvis tight, she would lift the springs from her legs. She would stretch, stretch, maintain a perfect slant, keep the head relaxed, look forward . . . concentrate.

That was the secret of the Ron Fletcher Method: concentration. Ron, a former dancer, had opened this tiny class—he called it, "body contourology"—one flight up on Wilshire, right next to the Beverly Hills Brown Derby. The studio was small, with chocolate walls and lots of hanging plants. You could almost pretend you were in Paris or New York. The dressing room was a curtain stretched over one curved rod. It was, as Ali said, a *real* method. "It really worked. I would come out of there absolutely tingling . . . feeling just, well, *marvelous.*"

Going Hollywood

Everyone loved Ali. Novelist Gail Parent called her "the most popular girl in the class." Not that it was really a class; it was more like eight individual units, each one squeaking on her own tension-sprung slant board, each one with her legs locked into leather straps. Making figure-eights, trying to concentrate, making sure the board doesn't make noise, keeping that pelvis tight.

And the long, lanky girl—could she really be turning thirty-seven in April?—would stroll in, tired from the drive, her faded jeans covering her red leotards and black tights. She would frown almost subliminally. Why did she have to wait, hadn't she made an appointment? Then she would smile again; the afterimage of annoyance would disappear. She was, after all, the most popular girl in the class, the nicest person anyone had ever known, always encouraging someone, always putting herself down.

Until it became impossible. The concentration—how could you do it right when someone on the next board was talking about a six-figure deal while her pectorals twitched from the strain? Remembering that, Ali's voice tightened. If you closed your eyes and just listened, she sounded like . . . someone familiar. "Well, I mean I love Ron's, I really do, I mean I was the one who sent him just about everyone in the first place. But for me to have to call up and make an appointment? It used to be you could just drop in from wherever you were in Beverly Hills. But the last time I went, Tatum O'Neal was on one of the boards, seeing if this was the right kind of exercise for her. It made me sick, absolutely sick, the whole star thing. I couldn't stand it, it was so boring, but you must tell Ron hello for me next time you see him. I really do love him. It's just that whole other trip made me totally sick . . ." And as she says this, you think, who does this tough little Wellesley voice remind me of? Ah, it comes in a rush. Underneath the modulation, the educated tones, is the hint of a whine. Too refined to be kvetchy, but still, not much humor there. Of course: Brenda Patimkin.

No more Ron Fletcher's, then. Now we see her walking up the sidewalk on Bedford Drive on her way to the analyst's office, a walk she takes every weekday. One spots her by chance, her mouth set, her face studying the sidewalk, her eyes hard, her mouth unsmiling. She's beginning to look her age, someone whispers. Maybe it's because she's thinner than ever before; McQueen, Ali tells friends, makes her stay at skin-and-bones. (Yet he tips the scales at two hundred; his tastes run to beer and Mexican food.) At the Polo Lounge, people are half a beat late in recognizing them, they are so close to being parodies of themselves. McQueen strolls through the room first, faded work shirt tucked into dirty beige jeans, his feet in chukka boots, his beer gut leading the way. His beard is shaggy now, the skin is pale, the blond hair is shot with gray. He moves so quickly there's no chance to flash on his electric blue eyes. Anyway, people are looking at the girl behind him, her hair in a gypsy scarf, her endless legs in tight jeans, a nubby fisherman's sweater giving her the illusion of bulk. Ali whispers to the maître d', "In the back, we'd like a table in the back." His Of-course-Miss-MacGraw booms over the front tables. Now heads turn. Is it Ali? At first no one is sure. It's been so long, her career is so "cold," people have heard that she's in hiding, gone back to the earth; isn't she more into health foods at the beach house? Like vultures, they look for signs of decay, of weakness. Is it, they wonder, finally getting to her?

It may be. When Ryan O'Neal pulled up alongside the

brown Mercedes at a red light in Beverly Hills not long ago, it took him a second to realize that the angry-looking girl, her hands tight on the wheel, was his *Love Story* co-star. He smiled. Sealed behind electric windows, she missed it. He tapped on the glass. The dark-haired girl stared at him. She had no idea who he was. "Hey, remember me? Ryan? We made a movie together," he joked. Of course. "Ryan, how are you? I was just thinking about you. I just read something about you in *Women's Wear,* didn't I?" O'Neal started to answer. The light changed. Ali's turn to smile: "Gee, I've got to go. But it's been super seeing you." The brown Mercedes became a dot disappearing down Sunset.

Friends explain Ali this way: If she's not always happy, at least she's in love. And what love! "You've never seen two people more obviously into one another," says *Getaway* producer David Foster. "They're just like a couple of kids. All over each other." He should know. *The Getaway* was where the unmaking of Ali MacGraw began. And in El Paso, of all places, thousands of miles from the mansion with eighteen rooms and twenty-six phones that Ali had given as her address for almost three years. That dream house on Woodland Avenue—good enough for almost any other princess—may have been home to Bob Evans. But for Ali MacGraw? A friend once said that if she checked into a motel, she'd bring her own prints to hang on the walls, she'd tie the drapes back in a special knot. When Ali MacGraw teamed up with Bob Evans, she never changed an ashtray. Never rearranged a stick of furniture or fussed with the bachelor browns, never had a Bernard Buffet switched from one room to another, never had the mirrors over the tub removed, never called the decorator about the lush pale-blue silk curtains in the bedroom. In short, Ali never moved in.

Why should she? She knew she wasn't going to stay.
Oh, not consciously. But underneath, where she lived in
fantasy, Bob Evans was just one more stone on her private yellow brick road.

The road started in Pound Ridge, an elegant patch of
"country" near New York. But, Ali explained, "we had
rather little money. My parents were both artists." Commercial artists: Frances MacGraw specialized in children's books, her husband was a nonprofessional archi-
tect. Ali and her brother spent the winters in front of the
fireplace, surrounded by books. "We were very, very
loved." Ali thrived in that climate; she became, she said,
"a terrific student, a very aggressive little girl, and a
righteous student leader." She proved that at Rosemary
Hall, a posh prep school in nearby Greenwich. A scholarship student, she made straight A's, and spent a lot of
time by herself, thinking private teenage thoughts. She
walked through this picture postcard of a school with its
Tudor buildings, gray stone, and that marvelous steeple.
Years later, when she was debating whether to accept a
commercial for Love cosmetics, she'd think of that steeple again. Love was offering $100,000, and Rosemary
Hall was moving to a new campus. The money, Ali
thought, could be used to move the steeple. "When I was
growing up," she rhapsodized, "I probably learned more
from that steeple, just sitting there, reflecting, than at
any other time in my life. If I ever got a lot of money,
what I would want to do is have it moved to the new
campus so I could give some other girl the same opportunity to sit and stare at the steeple for hours at a time,
thinking about life." Ali would accept the Love commercial; the steeple would stay on the old campus.

After Rosemary Hall came Wellesley. Ali was still on
scholarship but she was beginning to degawk, beginning

to turn into the girl she had always wanted to be. She made the cover of the *Mademoiselle* college issue. The smile was genuine. The crooked tooth (the modeling agencies would turn her down for years because of it) was hidden by the camera angle. She wore a skampie, a wool skirt divided up the center, and a burnt-orange mohair sweater. This girl *couldn't* be fat. You'd have to flip to the Alice MacGraw cartoon inside ("How I Diet") to see the whimsical portrait of a mini-blimp hopping on and off a scale.

And then she was cast in *All's Well That Ends Well.* Robin Hoen was also in it. He'd met her before, when he and a photographer friend went hunting for beautiful college girls to feature in the *Ivy League Guide.* Ali was the prettiest, the brightest, and the nicest. Hoen's opinion counted; he was Harvard, tall, the son of a famous neurosurgeon, headed for a solid career at the Chase Manhattan. Erich Segal, another member of the cast, was obscure beside Hoen.

After graduation, Ali went to work for the venerable Diana Vreeland. It was fifty dollars a week and a lot of pencil-sharpening, but for a first job it was an extraordinary break, a real acknowledgment of her potential. She was ready to marry Robin Hoen. Already she had incredible flair. No Bradford Bachrach wedding pictures for her—she flipped through *Vogue,* looking for something special, something romantic, with antiques and dreams. The credit on those photographs read "Melvin Sokolsky." He was famous. The worst he could say was no. He said no; he just couldn't take wedding pictures, don't be ridiculous. Ali wanted to come over and talk about it.

She stood in the doorway of Sokolsky's studio, the freshest-faced twenty-one-year-old anyone had seen in years. Sokolsky recorded the Hoen-MacGraw merger.

He brought more than his camera. "Whatever Mrs. Vreeland is paying you, I'll double it," he offered. "Come work as my stylist." In 1961, she did. And New York opened to her; Sokolsky's studio was like a discothèque where the city's brightest stars danced. They adored Ali. "We used to get jobs just because she was our stylist," a former employee remembers. You could not help but love her. Warmth like this had to be genuine. It was. They wanted more. But she was married to a banker. An anomaly. Yes, but so was she: Hoen described her in this "highly motivated and fast-moving set" as "socially uncomfortable, her own nature is private, meditative." Very much so, apparently; Ali has never acknowledged the existence of this happy time in print.

Then she met Henry Wolf. Older, maybe forty-one, a Middle European photographer whose work was just about everywhere you looked. He was the gateway to another New York: dinners at "21," rides around town in his sportscar with a scarf knotted around his neck. Ali and Robin divorced; later she would say that "he was perfectly nice, we had nothing in common." She would never mention him again. She was moving faster now. A year with Henry Wolf. Promotion from assistant to actual fashion stylist. She was making perhaps $25,000 a year. *New York* featured her as a girl with an interesting job. She kept her eyes open. And what she saw was her boss, Jordan Kalfus, Mel Sokolsky's partner. He was dark, sensual, and his limpid brown eyes could knock anyone over. And he was young. Ali left Henry Wolf and moved in with Kalfus.

She was getting restless; she wanted the fun of being in front of the camera. But she was too good at what she did, styling the models, finding the trinkets used in the pictures ("I could still tell you where to find just about anything in all of New York"), and the modeling agencies were turning her down. Lose weight, they said. Too Spanish. Crooked teeth. She worked harder at being beautiful; she already was, undeniably, the nicest girl anyone knew. She filled books with drawings for holiday presents, "surrounding everything with beauty," a former boyfriend remembers. It began to pay off: The Chanel ad, with Ali under a waterfall, shone with a vitality that vibrated right off the gloss.

"I passed that drugstore window every day for a year. I'd walk by just to see the picture. She was the most beautiful woman I'd ever seen," a former Ashley-Famous agent recalls. He tried finding her. None of the model agencies listed her. He located her through a Chanel account executive. Ali MacGraw answered the phone: "Mel Sokolsky's studio." She was flattered, but no, she liked what she was doing, and she didn't want to be an actress if she couldn't be "the best." When she paid him a courtesy call at the agency, people stared. Who was that girl?

She was not, she made clear, a cliché, not another pop model turned actress. She sensed a change; the go-go years for models were almost over. She enrolled in acting classes, and kept the agent's card.

If Phase One was Robin Hoen and Phase Two was Henry Wolf–Jordan Kalfus, then Phase Three for Ali MacGraw was Robin Clarke. He came along naturally, a symbol of her development. She had come to acting late, she knew the others were better, and Robin could talk into the night about acting and feelings. The call to read for *Goodbye, Columbus* came too soon. Ali was scared. She'd been tested for only one movie. And she'd met Bob Evans once before. He'd said, "No style, I didn't like her at all." And now he was looking at her tests for this Paramount movie and calling her agent. "Congratulate her for me," he said. "She's going to be brilliant."

Not at first. Ali froze on the set, emergency meetings were called, another actress waited in the wings. And then it all got better: Ali became Brenda, her laughter bubbling onto the screen. Bob Evans watched the dailies in his inky projection room, three thousand miles away. The girl was magic. He was right. More: He was in love. But every time he phoned Ali, asking about a New York lunch, she'd say no thanks or, worse, Robin and I would love to. He'd say, But I'm the head of the studio, I want to discuss your next film. She'd say, Thanks for thinking of me, send it to my agent.

No one wanted *Love Story* in the beginning. "Too Jewish," Bob Evans decided. "Change it." They did. The only remaining problem was to find a director who'd be good for Ali. Evans tricked Ali into flying alone to Los Angeles to see a rough-cut of Arthur Hiller's new movie. Don't worry, she told Robin, I'll be back tomorrow. Evans met her at the plane. David, whom Joyce Haber calls "the best butler in America," served dinner. After supper they watched the film, ate mints, drank wine. They took a midnight swim. Ali never went back to New York.

Joyce Haber called Evans to tease him: "Bob, everyone says you're getting married, is it true?" The seemingly permanent bachelor answered her seriously: It was for real. The magazines had a field day. It was the studio head and the star, a media dream. But the wedding was human, simple, Ali-like; she carried a hand-picked bouquet of azaleas she'd filched from a nearby garden. Ten days later, she started filming *Love Story.*

"Can you believe I had no idea anything was going

on?" says *Love Story* director Arthur Hiller. "And even to this day, I'm surprised." The set was filled with talk of Ali and Ryan's affair, but Ali never acknowledged the rumors, never let on. Soon it wouldn't matter. At the end-of-shooting party in spring, 1970, Ali MacGraw wrapped her cape around her and vanished alone into the night while her co-star sat dumbfounded.

What Evans thought would be a nice little film turned out to be Paramount's life preserver. *Love Story* opened at Christmas, with Ali heavily pregnant but otherwise unchanged. She made sure there were pine cones and velvet on the old-fashioned tree; she bought a caftan for Paramount publicity head, Marilyn Stewart. At the premiere, she was madonna-like in royal-blue panne, with a sequined skullcap for accent.

It was like a fairy tale, but even fairy tales change. Evans was working on *The Godfather.* He was always working now, always away. In Car City, Ali was stranded; she'd never learned how to drive. There were other signs. One night when Bob was out of town, Ali had supper with friends in the tiny alcove off the kitchen. She picked up a bell and laughed, "I never thought I'd get used to ringing this thing." Later, when David forgot the mustard, she rang for him. When he failed to appear, she rang it again. A line of petulance marked her brow before she remembered who she was and relaxed.

She didn't so much cross a line as get pulled over it. The *Time* cover, Joshua's birth, her busyness with the baby, her refusal to let him be photographed, her very private privacy—she didn't really create all that, it happened to her, happened around her. Because there was this enormous demand for who she was. Almost against her will, there was an Ali industry. People were hired at Paramount just to find scripts for her. She rejected them

all. She said she would "never spend more than three
months away from my family."

She never had a chance. Hollywood doesn't understand *no;* her agent, Sue Mengers, who was coincidentally Bob Evans's best friend, would have socked her
client into a Michael Caine spy film if the deal were sweet
enough. The world's about work, and words like "nee-
dlepoint" and "the baby" are treasonous when you
haven't worked in a year.

Then Bob Evans hurt his back playing tennis and was
glued to his bed for months. He could barely sit up for
an hour; a hospital bed was moved into the Paramount
screening room. The baby was spending more time with
his nanny. Ali took refuge at the Sanctuary, a now-
defunct health club where the stars worked out and
talked deals. "I never really wanted to be an actress," Ali
had once said. But it was too late; now she was a star, and
the computers decreed the company needed more Mac-
Graw product. Because of the computers and the accountants, Ali MacGraw was asked to play a Texas gun
moll opposite Steve McQueen.

She hated *The Getaway* on sight. She had other plans
—for *The Great Gatsby.* Daisy was her literary self-image,
the capper of her career. She nagged Paramount for two
years; she convinced Evans it had to be *Gatsby.* Paramount bought the rights, but they liked the *Getaway*
script more, and anyway, the cash flow was low; *The Godfather* was still in production.

Evans invited McQueen and director Sam Peckinpah
to dinner. She still said no. Sue Mengers, Ali and Bob's
dear friend, turned to a fellow agent and said, "You
know, it used to be that when a script was sent to me for
Ali, it was clean. No butter stains. No fingerprints. I don't
get them that way any more." Bob was sick that Christ-

mas; Ali changed his nickname from "Evans" to "Baby." They went to Acapulco, where, Ali told friends later, Gulf + Western conglomerate chief Charles Bluhdorn called her to say: "If Bob doesn't make this movie at Paramount, he'll lose his job."

McQueen took the film to First Artists, his own company, but something was clicking in Ali. By March she had signed for *The Getaway* and was working with McQueen. Anyone watching the first weeks of rushes could tell they were in love. "I would rather trust one of the mechanical sharks in *Jaws* than Ali MacGraw," Joyce Haber said later. This was a scandal: the wife of the studio head openly cuckolding him with her new co-star. Six weeks later, Evans flew to the set, but it was too late. This wasn't just any star, this was everyone's macho fantasy, this was back-to-basics, a man on a motorcycle cutting through hills, or, as *The New York Times* had once called him, "the vroom-vroom kid."

If Ali forgot Evans, she remembered *Gatsby*. Shooting was to start in Newport that summer. Bob and Ali went on a second honeymoon, to the Hotel DuCap. She didn't want to go, and Evans had scheduled a two-month trip. Later it would be reported that Steve had given her an ultimatum: Be back in a month. There were phone calls back and forth, but Ali, ever private, denied everything.

Evans had an ultimatum for her, too. He was postponing *Gatsby* for a year—the official announcement would say there were "weather problems"—and if she stayed with him, she'd be in the movie. If not . . . For Ali, Camelot had crumbled. There was no final scene, no confrontation. The morning she left, Bob told his good friend, Rona Barrett, they had made love and she had kissed him good-bye. When he came home, she was gone.

That was the summer of '72. *The Getaway* opened at Christmas; fueled by the publicity, it made $18 million. But Ali had bombed, and badly. Pauline Kael wrote, "The audience had a good time hooting at her, loved it when he smacked her face . . . Last time I saw Candice Bergen, I thought she was a worse actress than Mac-Graw. Now I think I slandered Bergen." It was public humiliation for the private girl; her ambition had out-stripped her simple wish to be the woman behind the man, and she'd lost control, falling into the public's affections only to discover that the masses were fickle. At the beach, at the analyst's, Ali is pinched, tight. Has she become Ibsen's Nora?

Not quite yet. She takes pleasure in simple cooking: tuna and steaks. McQueen makes her do the housework (the cleaning woman comes only once a week); presumably she savors that domesticity. Last June, with the desert sun baking Palm Springs, Steve and Ali trekked off alone to his house there and plastered and wallpapered; McQueen saw no reason to spend money on something they could do together. Joshua stayed with Bob Evans. ("Why do you call your ex-husband Bob Evans?" someone asked her recently. "Because," Ali said before she turned away, "that's his name.") She gave McQueen an antique motorcycle for Christmas; when she tries to talk about her favorite authors in his presence, he cuts her off. "Nobody's interested," he says. And he makes fun of her, calls her "nub knees." Sometimes Ali laughs. At Big Sur over Labor Day, Ali and Diane von Furstenburg lay side by side on chaise longues, topless. McQueen slouched by. "Four bee stings," he joked. Ali reportedly pouted for hours.

As she describes her life, it sounds dull: "I look forward to dressing up." Those occasions are fewer and

Going Hollywood

fewer. Still, Sue Mengers calls often. McQueen says Ali will work with him or not at all. The scripts are rejected out of hand. *Missouri Breaks* was written for them, but when director Bob Rafelson learned that Ali was part of the package, he balked. He wanted "a real actress," he said. Rafelson was bought out. Marlon Brando was brought in.

Where do you see Ali MacGraw these days? In cowboy restaurants with McQueen. Maybe at Sue Mengers's house for dinner with best friend, Candy B. Or driving in Steve's van, with the cycles in back. Or, mostly, at home, where *paparazzi* sneak pictures of her, a solitary figure on a porch.

The golden girl? She's burrowed in, watching the burnish fade. The days have come full circle, and she's aware of it; she says she's content to stay at home, happy to sign her name "McQueen." The fantasy has yet to wear thin. "Do I feel victimized by the system out here?" Ali repeated, considering my question for the briefest instant. "No, I don't. Hollywood has a way of saying, we love you, we destroy you, then we rediscover you . . . and you either get resurrected or you don't."

Somewhere there is a movie for her. A new director, a new producer, an international star. The answer to the question, whatever happened to Ali MacGraw? is not, finally, that she's waiting to be resurrected. Ali MacGraw will resurrect herself. It's her next Phase. Like a great athlete, she is holding on, running low, looking for her opening. And then, inevitably, moving on. Is Ali MacGraw, in that tired Hollywood phrase, "over"? Never. With Ali MacGraw, the jury is always out.

HOLLYWOOD, UNCOVERED

Götterdämerung, they tell you, is when no one will take your calls. "What do you want to do, turn out like Bill Davisson [*TV Guide*]? *Nobody* takes his calls any more." The eyebrows climbing toward the ceiling and the creeping contempt belonged to a Twentieth Century–Fox producer. He was willing to take my calls, but then, he was also willing to have me sign a two-page agreement from his lawyer which would have allowed him to retain the rights to his entire interview. "For insurance purposes," he explained.

He's not the only player in Hollywood who acts as if the interviewing process is as sacred as a deal memo. "Pick your enemies carefully—or you'll never make it in this town," Rona Barrett once advised *Village Voice* writer Blair Sabol. And, as ubiquitous agent Sue Mengers lectured Sabol and myself on separate occasions, "Rex Reed came out here to write hatchet jobs until no one would take his calls, so he had to go back to New York and become a film critic." Seeing my astonishment at this revelation—Rex Reed labors under the impression that he is one of Sue Mengers's closer friends—she hurriedly amended that. "I mean, he was accepted by *the community,* but only after he wrote a few good pieces. "

Its studios' labs may have perfected the Technicolor

process, but "the community's" views on journalism are still black-and-white. And while a Sue Mengers may not be making as many deals in the new, product-scarce Hollywood, her analysis of the status of print media is right on the money: So far as "the business" is concerned, reportage breaks down neatly into "nice pieces" and "hatchet jobs."

No one really disagrees with Mengers's assessment of what constitutes a good piece—"Most journalism in Hollywood is pure puffery," says Los Angeles *Times* assistant arts editor Wayne Warga. What's even more depressing is that no one defends what Mengers and her pack call hatchet jobs by insisting they be called by a fairer name: possibly "serious reporting" on subjects that Hollywood would rather ignore.

Why do there seem to be so few serious journalists in Hollywood? The awards system is one reason. Each year the Publicists Guild of America hands out equivalents of the Pulitzer Prize for "Best Coverage of Hollywood." Publicists handing out Pulitzers! Charles Champlin of the Los Angeles *Times,* Army Archerd of *Daily Variety,* Vernon Scott of UPI, Jim Bacon of the *Herald Examiner,* and Bosley Crowther of *The New York Times* have all accepted their plaques with thanks. Apparently the competition isn't exactly fierce. With the exception of the Reuters man, the foreign press is so moribund it's been nicknamed the Hollywood Press Corpse.

The national media isn't much better. A member of one newsweekly's L.A. bureau told me, "When I first moved out here, I was deeply disappointed that I never got a phone call thanking me for an article." And over at the other weekly, a regular on the show-business beat buttonholed me to complain: "I don't know why I'm the one who has to endure those lunches with people like

Burt Reynolds bitching to me about the media treatment they're getting from everybody else."

I know why Burt Reynolds chose his companion, but I sure don't know how the star's complaints could fill an entire lunch hour. Serious reporting is rarely done, yet a single well-placed and well-timed piece of journalism —invariably dismissed as a hatchet job by the "victim" —can insure temporary notoriety for a writer. Andrew Tobias's "The Apprenticeship of Frank Yablans" in *New York* (fall, 1974) still known as "the article," was talked about well into the winter. Pauline Kael's diatribe against the mentality of the New Hollywood prompted favorable replies from dozens of people it implicitly attacked, placing Kael right on target for someone else's exposé even as it guaranteed Kael some long-desired superstardom.

It's difficult to work in Hollywood without being compromised—or at least being aware of the opportunities. Every assignment begins the same way: with a tacit understanding between journalist and subject that for the duration of the story they're best friends. All articles start out as good pieces. A hatchet job is a betrayal of confidence. Publishers are said to rewrite an author's prose to suit their own bias.

The first time I did a piece in Hollywood, this process was unknown to me. I thought I was there to unravel the Byzantine story of Jon Peters's coming-to-power in the Barbra Streisand remake of *A Star Is Born.* I went up to Peters's Malibu ranch to get his story. As he walked me through the garden that Streisand had planted for him, Peters began by suggesting that if this piece worked out well I could become the official Streisand-Peters chronicler and tell their continuing story in *McCall's, Redbook,* and *Playboy.* A month later, when, as we had agreed, I showed him his quotes, Peters threatened both me and

New Times with a lawsuit that he promised would set a new record for damages.

A few months later, Tom Laughlin was passing our interview time by reminding me that *Billy Jack Magazine* was his next fantasy and that I might get the nod to edit this prestigious journal. That is, after I finished the script he wanted me to write. But even before that article was finished, the moody Laughlin was kneading the bones of my neck as if determining how much pressure it would take to shatter them. He wasn't too proud to pick up the phone. "Whatever it takes to get you, I'll do it," he said.

They let you in and then, when they sense they may be betraying themselves, they betray you with double fervor. Blair Sabol was accosted by one of the Ikettes after her *Esquire* piece about Ike and Tina Turner last year: "I'm gonna smash your face in." Allan Carr has threatened her with death. When I asked *New West* film critic Steven Farber, whose personal taste in films is generally opposed to whatever other critics are praising, if he'd ever been threatened with extinction, he couldn't have been more bored. "Yes, the director and editor of *Jaws* did say something like that after my piece in *The New York Times,* but I knew it didn't mean anything."

And he's right: It's just idle bluster, it means nothing. After all, it's not like the East Coast, where journalists can topple a government or expose government abuse. This is only Hollywood, where even the hatchet jobs, in the larger order of things, hardly stir a palm frond. Jon Peters's version of *A Star Is Born* did get made; Tom Laughlin enjoyed a year of grace after my piece was published, making still more grandiose plans for his media empire; Allan Carr transformed himself from a talent manager to a full-fledged producer. Granted, after the Tobias devastation of Frank Yablans, which preceded Yablans's firing by scant weeks, the Hollywood soothsayers did declare Yablans out for the count. But Yablans picked himself up, produced *Silver Streak* (gross to date: $55 million), and inspired a wave of articles about his rise from the tomb.

In the cosmic order of things, whether Frank Yablans produces the $55-million triumph or some other producer pulls the brass ring hardly seems like high-stakes action, but only the failures in Hollywood invoke the cosmic order; like the Old Hollywood, the new kids in town are delighted to witness the restoration of a Frank Yablans, as if Yablans's comeback preserves a kind of natural balance. It is considered bad form to question whether their entire world is worth preserving.

God knows the players certainly don't. Locked into the mind-set of survival at any cost, they are even prepared to love their detractors. Paradoxically, the correct response to a hatchet job can be masochistic "You're so right, why didn't I ever see it?" praise for the writer. This is a reaction Hollywood has perfected over the years, the inspiration for this tradition coming from Louis B. Mayer and his experience with Lillian Ross. Before Ross was allowed to publish *Picture,* her revealing and wart-filled portrait of Mayer, she was obligated to show it to the studio chief. If Mayer refused to approve it, her *New Yorker* piece was dead, so naturally Ross was worried that all her labor was in vain. She needn't have fretted. Mayer loved the Ross profile. Not only did it confirm some inner view he had of himself, but it told the world that he was a despot who didn't mind excoriation, and Mayer was shrewd enough to realize that at a certain level there's no such thing as bad publicity. Not long ago, Julie Baumgold profiled Robert Evans for *New West,* and though her Stahr-like portrayal of a man whose career flourished in spite of his inability to sustain a satisfying relationship was a dizzying portrait of Hollywood disconnection, it was intended to show Hollywood's last Fitzgerald character at his best. To many readers, the vision of Evans alone in bed, his Valium and Beluga caviar within arm's reach, was more than disconcerting, but Evans was obviously pleased—he ordered twenty-six copies of the magazine shipped to friends.

Evans and Mayer were both right. The most laudatory and the most vitriolic articles have the same effect: a confirmation of the subject's importance, an ironic validation that in Hollywood the most important of the writer's tasks is making sure the names are spelled right. What is written, in the long run, is considered less important than that *something* was written; all the reader is assumed to retain is the impression that the subject is that uniquely American aristocrat, the bona fide celebrity. What the celebrity did to win our attention, how he or she intends to hold on to it—those are niceties, of no real significance. And with the convertible top down, the radio playing an unbroken string of Southern California hits, the sky over San Vicente Boulevard a mind-stopping blue, the role of watcher-at-the-gates even takes on a certain logic. Often journalists are merely recording the treadmarks of those who, as Daniel J. Boorstin put it, "are well-known for their well-knownness." In that spirit, the recognition that what passes for normal life here can be wildly aberrant is only icing on the cake for those reporters lucky enough to spend a few years in the sun.